Uta Brandes
Sonja Stich
Miriam Wender

Design by Use

The Everyday Metamorphosis of Things

Birkhäuser
Basel · Boston · Berlin

Contents

Transition and Experience as Perspectives of Design Research

What has long been considered a foregone conclusion in other areas of research is today also true for design: the proof of the pudding is in the eating. It is no longer sufficient to merely indulge in either general or specific meta-discussions on methodologies or even on the fundamental question as to whether design is at all qualified to undertake research. As important as these issues may be, what is needed now is the publication of relevant results from design research.

Such results and research have existed for quite some time and they demonstrate how distinctive and radical design research is and can be. This study and its theoretical reflections are a case in point.

It is particularly worth mentioning that this research work uses diverse methodologies from the social and cultural sciences (without specifically referring to them at all times) and by interweaving them develops new dimensions of research. Most importantly, however, a specific quality of design in relation to research is taken up here: the ability to analyse situational contexts in a transitory way, to fathom the interwoveness and in-betweeness of theory and practice, and to take seriously the history of objects and their use as a competence and a quality. Thus this study substantiates a systematic analysis of the relationship between design (*Entwurf*) and empirical use and, in so doing, also examines research methodologies and opportunities as well as the dimensions of design within the framework of everyday culture.

Another aspect is also noticeable: this study deliberately forgoes the generally accepted assumption or expectation that one must and should present results of a 'precise' quality in the traditional sense. Instead, and almost en passant, as it were, this work discusses and explains the quality of fuzziness as an essential means of insight and of design research.

The manner of representation in this piece of research, as an aside, not only communicates but also in and of itself creates and extends reflection and insight.

All this and much more you will find in this excellent example of design research and in its considerations, discussions, and results.

Board of International Research in Design, BIRD

Fluid Design
& Research

Design as Research Paradigm

The area of design research has experienced some rather intense disputes concerning the definition and evaluation of theoretical and investigative approaches, but this is still a fairly young phenomenon. During the development of design into a specialist area in its own right, the concept of design research was – if at all – put into practice, explained in terms of cultural history, or ideologised around functionality for the benefit of knowledge creation in technological or engineering contexts. Mostly, however, science was (and partly still is) understood as something other than, and certainly not inherent to, design. In particular in the German design tradition, design was seen as *Entwurf* (a term that is difficult to translate into other languages but roughly equates to "blueprint", "sketch", "draft") and therefore as something tied to practice. Although each *Entwurf* needs prior research in order to mature into a finished product, sign or service, this has not been considered research in the proper scientific sense, not least due to the fact that different approaches were used than those already established in traditional scientific research. It is hard to think of any other academic discipline that has to confront such outright scepticism towards its research potential and regarding the question as to whether it could actually be truly scientific. This scepticism is not only articulated by "established" sciences and researchers but is also reproduced by some designers and design faculties. A popular expression used to deny design any competence in terms of science and research is the hastily produced subaltern reference to some ominous "eye-level" with other sciences, which design has not yet reached – sometimes with a subtext indicating the general futility of such an endeavour. Another, not quite unproblematic, evaluation of the scientific capabilities of design is based on Niklas Luhmann's strategies for the reduction of complexity and used to present design as the model discipline for the reduction of complexities in this context: "Reduction of complexity is – design. Design consists of patterns of selection [...]. The difference between design and simplification is that design does not negate or destroy options, but instead selects either this or that option on a case-by-case basis."[1]

A case-by-case selection is at least better than destruction. What remains, however, is the danger of contingency not just in the sense of the possible but also, obviously, the accidental or arbitrary.

Wolfgang Jonas, on the other hand, identified design as a "fuzzy term"[2]. And correctly so because the nature of design is its "in-betweeness": between theory and – according to Michel de Certeau[3] – "practice". It is exactly the "fuzziness" of this in-betweeness that, far from the conventional self-degradations of a simplistic "eye level", distinguishes design from the traditional sciences. In short: the traditional sciences are burdened by the frozen norms of so-called "scientific standards" while design theory and research, with

---

1   Holger van den Boom, 'Design als dritte Kultur', in *Öffnungszeiten. Papiere zur Designwissenschaft*, 21, (Lübeck, 2007), p. 7.

2   Cf. Uta Brandes, Wolfgang Jonas, and Meyer Voggenreiter, 'Zum Designforschungsbegriff in der DGTF. Ein Annäherungsversuch aus 3 Richtungen.' in *Design Report*, 1/2 (2007).

3   Cf. Michel de Certeau, *Kunst des Handelns* (Berlin, 1988).

their far lighter baggage of modernism, are able to offer a confident and critical debate, which other disciplines might well use to further and re-think their understanding of research.

The fact that design is continuously oscillating between action (practice) on the one hand, and theory and research on the other – meaning between concrete everyday life and traditional scientific thinking, both of which influence and change each other – has to be considered an opportunity.

Design as a Transitory Discipline

To restate the above: design theory and research as independent areas of inquiry are still in their infancy even if related discussions, papers and conferences have seen a clear increase throughout the last few years. Where efforts in this direction are under-taken, theory and research swiftly look to other areas such as aesthetics, cultural and social studies, or economy to name but a few. This is problematic in so far as present results have mainly consisted of contingent wish lists, have produced disparate ap-proaches, which can at best be described as exchangeable parts that remain discon-nected and unrelated.

In the necessary attempt to endow the discipline with a profile befitting an evolved modernism which simultaneously takes into account design's particular position as a transitory area between science and "action", the question remains as to whether de-sign theory and research are at all able to exist in isolation. One hypothesis has stated that the specific quality of design might lie in its contribution to the general study of everyday life, culture and economy, which could change, extend and qualify the fabric of the established sciences.

The authors of this book understand the particular positioning of design as a transitory entity as an opportunity to undertake a reification of the empirical. Contrary to the discourse of constructivism, we have placed the empirical at the centre of our analysis as a re-discovered and different form of observation in the sense of "facts of experience", which has been in danger of disappearing from sight in the face of a pref-erence for meta-theoretical methodologies. Accessing the empirical via precise obser-vation and perception as well as the resulting theses for the creation and production of objects and their use might help to provide new insights into, and interpretations of, everyday life. "The only remedy is perception as passion, an embodied thinking, which started as a thinking against thinking and which now follows hard on the heels of those effects that have come about through the suicidal installation of a sitting subject."[4]

---

4   Dietmar Kamper, 'Entweder der Sinn oder die Sinne', in *Der Sinn der Sinne*, ed. Kunst- und Ausstellungshalle der Bundesrepublik Deutschland (Bonn, Göttingen, 1998), p. 16.

The Things in Design

The literature on things – as physical phenomena and material entities, as a category and as an irrefutable reference for the subject as well as its opposite – is incredibly diverse since no discipline of either science or art can do without an investigation into the world of objects, which simultaneously create and define conditions. "Man used to force his rhythm onto the objects, today however, it is the objects in their continuous movement, with their disordered appearance, their pressure and replacement, their constant impermanence, which force their rhythm onto man."[5]

Thus it would not be at all surprising if design in particular were to apply itself to the study of objects since observation and an understanding of the creation of the world of objects are part of its original assignment. Using the conjunctive form here, however, indicates that things are not quite that simple. For one thing, the history of design and design education, which can be astonishingly conventional, tend to reduce the discipline to a predominantly practice-oriented activity that is mostly targeted at the acquisition of technical skills and a refined awareness of aesthetic forms. If more comprehensive questions are integrated at all, they have, in recent times, usually focussed on categories of knowledge. The deficits in the study of design theory and research are further supported and aggravated by external perspectives: the expectations of design users and resellers, in particular of manufacturers, retailers and consumers. However, we can observe a slow disintegration of these traditional ideas and demands. And herein lies an opportunity for design. What is needed now is the establishment of an extended understanding of design: the broadening of the discipline into one that comprises theoretical studies and empirical research, and organisational and communicative competencies as implicitly as it includes the generation of design products. Design can, and must, acquire a position which enables it to act in a multi-disciplinary way and to provide fresh impulses for the analysis and study of everyday culture from the perspective of use.

Gert Selle and Jutta Boehe are among those few today who have formulated an interesting approach within the category of use: "There is a striking similarity between the strands of critical, functionalist, traditionalist, cynical and pure design theories. It is the negation of the user as the subject. A deficit in the study and theory of use has long been known without any recognisable professional efforts to close this gap through research and intellectual efforts. All the more assiduously market analysis jumps into the breach as a willing helper of science and informs us about buying incentives and behaviour."[6]

---

5   Jean Baudrillard, *Das System der Dinge* (Frankfurt, New York, 1991), p. 198.

6   Gert Selle and Jutta Boehe, *Leben mit den schönen Dingen. Anpassung und Eigensinn im Alltag des Wohnens* (Hamburg, 1986), p. 257.

The functions which have so far been assigned to use could be summarised thus:

- personal concepts of order within a collection of things
- possession of things as an act of control over them
- possibilities of interaction in social contexts through their possession
- symbolisation of meanings and memories

The Production of Things Through Use

"Non-Intentional Design" (NID) is the term that was agreed upon for this project. A term not yet to be found in general language, but which has recently debuted in an academic context[7] and which describes the everyday re-design of the designed world. Each everyday object, as long as it is not a product of nature, has been designed and manufactured. In the context of our study, questions of assignation and evaluations of aesthetic and functional qualities, design authorship (anonymous or personally branded design), types of production, areas and places of use as well as technological complexity are of no importance whatsoever. To put it more precisely: these considerations are only relevant from the perspective of possible ways of use.

"Each product, regardless as to whether it was intentionally designed or not, can trigger associations because it is solely dependent upon the social and cultural contexts which kind of associations the product will generate."[8]

This implies that ever since we have made objects our own, we have used them not only in traditional, but also in new contexts. This phenomenon points to an extraordinarily broad field of study that reaches far back into our past, as far as the beginnings of object culture. From the Stone Age onwards, if not earlier, humans have used materials found in nature for the improvement of survival strategies: using stones to make fire and to grind down hard foodstuffs, sharpening stones to use them as "knives" for scratching, splitting and cutting, using twigs as arrows, darts and skewers and so on. Thus the impulse to solve problems is connected to an ancient human ability to intrumentalise existing objects and conditions for our own ends.

These early periods of humanity, however, are not part of our study. The beginnings of Non-Intentional Design are closely linked to the development of a product culture which started during the later period of industrialisation. In other words, during a period which made it possible to manufacture things in series and as mass consumer goods and during which the new profession of the designer of technical products emerged as a profession in its own right, hereby differentiating itself from craftsmanship. Ever since then it has become increasingly obvious how the concepts

---

7   Cf. Uta Brandes, 'Non Intentional Design', in *Wörterbuch Design. Begriffliche Perspektiven des Design*, ed. Michael Erlhoff and Tim Marshall (Basle, Boston, Berlin, 2008), p. 291–293.

8   Uri Friedländer, 'Gedanken zum Thema "Produktsemantik"', in *Design und Identität*, ed. VDID (Düsseldorf, 1991/1992), p. 55.

When there is no bottle opener to hand – whether on the street or at a party –
a lighter can do the job.

of product definition and assignation can differ between designers and users. "I posit that they [the designers] know too little about the people for whom they design their products. How they live, what their true desires are and also what they definitely do not want. How could they? In their professional life, they have no direct contact with the consumer, they cannot directly influence him. At worst, between them and the person who selects and buys there are: hierarchies of decision making at the manufacturer's, the representative of the manufacturer, the procurement manager of the wholesaler, the procurement manager of the retailer, shop windows, brochures, catalogues, advertisements, magazines and finally the salesperson."[9]

It follows that Non-Intentional Design can only exist in those areas in which it breaks with pre-defined intentions or does not follow a pre-defined way of use. A stone, for instance, does not have to be re-designed if it is not to be used as a knife. On the other hand, a knife that does not work – hence does not cut – rids itself more instantly of its reason for being. This has become even more obvious with the development of technologically complex machines: The rusty ruins of machines in non-developed countries are silent witnesses for what becomes of our difficult products if the designer's intention to communicate the functionality and use of these appliances is not redeemed or understood.

A further escalation has been taking place in the age of medialisation and technologisation, in which the use of things has become increasingly abstract and increasingly time-consuming. Things are becoming harder to understand (black box effect), wrong use can lead to frustration and a growing social gap has emerged between naive and skilful use. Knowledge of human behaviour with regard to things can supply some crucial experience. Whereas "improper" use can still be functional when low-complexity products are concerned, or might even endow the object with added value, most high-tech appliances are not suited for NID.

After due consideration, we came to the conclusion that the coined term "Non-Intentional Design" was best suited to describe the phenomenon under investigation. However, "non intentional" must not be confused with "arbitrary, "meaningless", "aimless" or "not goal-oriented". The clear purpose of these instances of re-design is finding a solution to a problem. However, the desire to solve a problem can originate from various situations and motivations. It can be more or less spontaneous or might be implemented more or less deliberately. In order to unlock the semantics correctly, it should be mentioned, however, that the negating adjective "non intentional" refers, in any case, essentially to the subject. The emphasis of the subject is meant to underline the fact that the intention here is not to design something. There is no impulse to consciously create. Non-Intentional Design is neither defined by, nor infused with, the will to design. Thus, the users' motivation to use an object for a purpose other than that for which it was professionally intended is geared towards the elimination of a temporary or continuous deficit. On the other hand, an analysis of these acts shows – as will be demonstrated in this study – that this use contains a potential that can extend and

---

9   Josef Kremerskothen, 'Wegzeichen für eine Zeit, in der die Phantasie wieder eine Chance haben wird', in *form 96* (Frankfurt, 1981), p. 8 ff.

redefine the idea of design and that opens up new dimensions of everyday culture and the study thereof.

Non-Intentional Design defies all norms,[10] endows seemingly one-dimensional objects with a variety of (design) options, implies transformation in combination with clever new functionality. It arises from temporary situations of deficit, from convenience and from playfulness. It cuts costs and can reduce the overabundance of products. More often than not it is reversible or the used-up product finds a new and final purpose. NID describes what people do spontaneously and without any deliberate design intention because they are faced with a situational problem that they have or want to solve. Apparently, in these situations, structures of thought amalgamate in an associative, spontaneous way. They are triggered by the conditions and constructions defined by a particular situation and are eventually expressed in a permanent or occasional rule-breaking.

Non-Intentional Design thus studies the generation of the function or meaning of things in and through use. It describes all those actions, processes and ways of dealing with things where people change their living or working environment through minor or major interventions. The fact that professionally, and allegedly functionally, designed products and spaces are constantly re-designed, re-arranged or used differently points, on the one hand, to a lack of practical and theoretical observation and reflection of the empirical among design professionals. On the other hand, it serves as an indicator of the social problem regarding the limits or openness of designability. "In the context of design, ambiguity – if not understood as provocation – refers to an openness of the meaning of forms. [...] Forms of design have an a priori repertoire of meaning."[11]

Products and spaces, which – according to the criteria of professional design and its definition of meaningful use – are "misunderstood" or "abused", have a great potential for innovation and various new, other, multi-functional options of use. An analysis of the use of design products is so important not just because it is by using them, in the ways we deal with things, that cultural diversity and differences express themselves. The products themselves might increasingly be subject to globalisation – their use, however, creates differences.

---

10   Note that, if read backwards, the acronym NID becomes DIN (Deutsche Industrie Norm – German industry standard).

11   Gudrun Scholz, 'Wo bleibt der Designer? Über Identität und Pluralität', in *Design und Identität*, ed. Norbert Hammer and Birgit Kutschinski-Schuster (Düsseldorf, 1991/92), p. 63.

Relevance in Relation to Research

The metamorphosis of objects through use results in a number of questions relevant to research but also to methodology, which are both investigated in this publication: it is our clear intention that those are understood as exemplary approaches for design research. Without explicitly formulating the possible methodological approaches – be it in terms of a prismatic, hermeneutic, observational and photographic manner or through analogy … – these can nonetheless be found in the ways the material is collected, presented and analysed. We undertook a search for evidence (observational research) in people's everyday lives, we observed their actions in public spaces, at work, at home, in their spare time; we deliberately used a change of perspective and approached our subjects by looking at their actions. And conversely, we also investigated the conditions of the objects: their suitability regarding a potential for change, where the actual process of change was initiated by the intelligence, the anticipation and eventually the action of the users. We went from the microcosmic, the individual phenomenon, to the macrocosmic (a societal potential for imagination and creativity), from artful amateurism to professional design and anticipation, we combined micro and macro analyses and we included interculturality in terms of visual and theoretical aspects. In spite of a qualitative "fuzziness", we defined the borderlines of NID to other processes of "making a virtue out of necessity" that are evoked through different motivations. To sum up: In spite of its alleged normality, even banality and triviality, we respected the importance of everyday life (and the role of the people who live it) in that we argue for it constituting original design research. The seemingly trivial contains much of what defines observation in design.

Thus we are offering qualitative approaches which, on the scale of design research, are open-ended. They influence design in terms of concepts and as a practice and, ideally, change these aspects, as well as design research and theory, in productive ways because each question, and particularly each interest that seeks for insight, has an impact on the object. Research is a dynamic process which generates learning and insight and sets things in motion – if we allow this to happen instead of arguing for a positivistic pseudo-objectivity. On this basis we would like people to consider this type of design research, of understanding and concept of design as fluid design.

Explorations

From the enormous amount of available material dealing with the objects and the subjects, we have selected those publications for this book which are relevant for the NID project in a more direct sense. Categories such as use[12], user[13], participative design[14], open meaning,[15] and the role of the object[16] can mostly be found in design-related literature. Although they served us as important sources, they largely fail to provide any consequences or development options for another perspective in design research.

There are still surprisingly few approaches that touch on the phenomenon we call NID. Except for one instance, individual studies have emerged only recently which use terms such as "intuition", "rethinking", "improvisation" and which identify them as encapsulating potential qualities of human creativity. It is, however, striking that these publications have a rather strategic orientation or favour a practical discussion.

The only theoretical approach was formulated by Charles Jencks and Nathan Silver in the 1970s and termed "Adhocism": improvising by using arbitrary objects with the objective to satisfy a momentary need. However, they developed a one-dimensional connotation of Adhocism by linking this phenomenon to an anarchistic type of "self-realisation" of the subject when dealing with an otherwise alienated reality of things, and they describe these actions as a rare form of appropriation in the daily use of objects, thus an exception. With their intended misuse the users, according to Jencks and Silver, would deliberately ignore the intended use of an object, which appeared to be alien to them at that moment, in order to satisfy a personal need. [17]

So in spite of the clever term "Adhocism", its analysis is all but sound. In acts of improvisation the need for "self-realisation" does not trigger misappropriation – this would exactly presuppose an intention and thus a need for hobbyist tinkering. It is also wrong to state that Adhocism is an exception. On the contrary: everyone constantly "misappropriates" – as we will further elaborate empirically and theoretically – a variety of things, services, signs, and media.

---

12   "Thus an object can be used for totally different purposes from those it was intended and designed for. The designer might only be able to give an object some very general characteristics; the user takes over and designs himself [...]" – Gert Selle and Jutta Boehe, *Leben mit den schönen Dingen. Anpassung und Eigensinn im Alltag des Wohnens* (loc.cit.), p. 50.

13   "During the process of ideation it already becomes apparent that the interests of the user are not accounted for in the same way as those of the manufacturer. The user's everyday life is not considered as a source for inspiration." – Brigitte Wolf, *Design für den Alltag* (Munich, 1983), p. 98.

14   "In the modern world, participation cannot mean design without designers. It does not mean either that the designer is only the executor of the future user's will. We should rid ourselves of the expectation of being able to determine every detail from start to finish, of carrying everything through to perfection [...]. We suffocate from completeness." – Claude Schnaidt, in *Design-System-Theorie*, Wolfgang Jonas (Essen, 1994), p. 147.

15   See Gudrun Scholz, *Die Macht der Gegenstände. Designtheorie. 3 Essays* (Berlin, 1989), p. 42 ff.

16   "[...] in practice the object turns out to be the interface between changing roles. Seen in this light, the object cannot be assigned a particular role. Instead, the same object can take on different roles." – ibid., p. 36.

17   Cf. Charles Jencks and Nathan Silver, *Adhocism. The Case of Improvisation* (New York, 1993).

There is a second, more recent approach, which originates from the context identified earlier as strategic: Jane Fulton Suri is director of "Human Factors" at IDEO, one of the most renowned international design consultancies. IDEO stand out from other trend and futures consultancies because their methodologies for the study of everyday life often comprise unconventional, qualitative-empiricist methods. In a small volume mainly consisting of photographs, Fulton Suri compiles "those intuitive ways we adapt, exploit, and react to things in our environment; things we do without really thinking."[18] What is presented there as "intuitive design" is a fairly jumbled mixture of behaviours and habits in our everyday interaction with things. These interactions are identified through verbs that serve as questions: "reacting?", "responding?", "co-opting?", "exploiting?", "adapting?", "conforming?", and "signaling?".[19] Some of the photographs could easily be integrated into our analysis. They show, in terms of actions, the same changes in use that we encountered in everyday life (sitting on the steps of a stairway, skateboarding on low walls or curbs of squares etc.). However, Fulton Suri's interest in these human interactions focuses on a different aspect than that of NID: "Seeking inspiration from real life is a surprisingly obvious idea, but it is easily overlooked when we become preoccupied with our professional roles, with their traditional domains and established processes. [...] But for people who regard themselves as tasked with problem-solving or innovation, it is imperative to encourage and elevate the practice of observing everyday events."[20] She advocates awareness and refined observational skills in daily life in order to achieve new insights and solutions for her company from an understanding of the "normal", habitual and mundane actions of people. Her interest, therefore, originates from a pragmatic, instrumentalised professionalism with the intention of identifying new trends – albeit by using more suitable, hence qualitative-experimental, methods than usual – which are then profitably incorporated into her professional work. This is, of course, totally justified but it does not further the development of design research nor does it contribute to a greater awareness thereof.

---

18   Jane Fulton Suri & Ideo: *Thoughtless Acts? Observations on Intuitive Design* (San Francisco, 2005), interior dust jacket.

19   Ibid.

20   Ibid.

A View of
Other Disciplines

Use and Redefinitions of Use in Literature

The subject of Non-Intentional Design (NID) offers many interfaces with other areas of science and research. Since we were dealing with design in terms of concept and content, we started with a literature survey. Due to NID being a coined term we had to narrow down our search in a step-by-step process. As sources we used books on different subjects in design that touched on our topic.

A Synopsis of Design History from the Perspective of Use

Design as a profession is relatively young. However, in the – at most – 150 years of history of professional product design we can find different approaches and definitions as to what designers can do and what can be expected from design.

First attempts at a theoretical analysis of formgiving were developed at the Bauhaus. The social aspects of its teachings also had an impact on how the role of the user was understood: far from the fustiness of Biedermeier, the new functional forms should free not only the homes, but also the spirit, from any small-minded, petit bourgeois contents. The new forms, seen as harbingers of a new society, were not simply meant to be useful but also to educate. Options of use were limited by their design ("reduction to essentials") and steered utilisation towards pre-defined behaviours. Products such as Josef Albers' teacup, which required a way of drinking as from a tilting bucket, are an example for the strict, educational impetus of the Bauhaus masters. Here, the user was accounted for in the design process in a rather problematic way: as an executing entity. Free use, or even an emotional cathexis of objects, was not intended – besides their high price this is certainly one of the reasons why many designs from this period did not prevail.

As a countermovement to this functionalist approach, which was effectively – though not without contention – continued throughout the 1950s and 60s at the Ulm School of Design we can briefly look at the design movements around the "New Design"[21]. Throughout the 1960s, Italian designers were instrumental in advancing the debate in design. Based on a general dissatisfaction with the role of a mere henchman of industry, and thus as part of the production process of a market economy, a provocative design culture emerged, which produced statements rather than consumer goods. In the search for materials suitable for independent ideas, answers were found in the areas of industry and everyday life. For the first time, designers did not produce designs for industrial production, but instead used ready-mades from industrial production and incorporated them into their own products.

The relationship between object and user was about to change as well. Designing emotional products which would beyond mere functionality generate added value "for the soul" became one of the new guidelines. The process of making an object one's

---

21   Cf. Gudrun Scholz, 'Wo bleibt der Designer?', in *Design und Identität*, ed. Norbert Hammer and Birgit Kutschinski-Schuster, (loc.cit.).

own was thus already implicated in the design process itself, even if the otherwise rather quirky products left little room for ulterior uses. In comparison to the Bauhaus, which understood design as a method of social education, Italian design attempted to create new and unusual experiences in relation to objects.

In Germany different approaches also emerged outside industry, based on the radical concepts of Italian design. After the strict, minimalist product culture of the Ulm School, a new design movement developed throughout the 1980s, which was rougher and not quite as friendly as its Italian counterpart, but at least as experimental in using materials borrowed from other areas in its "Unikat Design".[22]

And there was also interaction with users. Only through use would the design process be completed, which, in other words, was an invitation for the laypersons to create their own designs. A typical product of this concept of design is "Sacco", a bean bag which only attains its essential form and function – be it as a seat, cushion or bed – through being used.

The Cultural History of Object Use

Besides the history of design itself, the cultural history of objects plays a significant role. The changing use of objects is closely intertwined with their development. Gert Selle[23] points out several times that objects have been subject to changes in meaning throughout the history of civilisation. Forms of utilisation are socially acquired behaviours and therefore respond to social change. Much could be learned from this source about the phenomenon of NID, if there were a scientifically documented history of objects. There are, however, two reasons as to why this intention is bound to fail: Firstly, in the context of NID, a history of objects is only of interest in as far as it considers the context of use, which in existing papers, in exhibitions and museums is largely neglected. Although the objects themselves might not have changed in their material properties, their use might well have undergone significant changes even if this is not documented anywhere. The second problem is an insufficient examination of everyday things, as Bazon Brock has noted.[24] Among other things, this is mainly due to "differentiating expressions of high culture from our everyday culture, thus focusing the methods of recording and analysis on the area of high culture."[25] Thus we have outstanding

---

22   Cf. HdK, Fachbereich 3, ed., *Kaufhaus des Ostens* (Berlin, 1984); Christian Borngräber, ed., *Berliner Design-Handbuch* (Berlin, 1987); Thomas Hauffe, *Fantasie und Härte. Das 'Neue deutsche Design' der achtziger Jahre* (Gießen, 1994); Wolfgang Schepers and Claudia Schneider-Esleben, ed., *Gefühlscollagen. Wohnen von Sinnen* (Cologne, 1986); Volker Albus and Christian Borngräber, *Design-Bilanz* (Cologne, 1992); Volker Albus, Monika Winkler, and Ursula Zeller, ed., *bewußt, einfach. Das Entstehen einer alternativen Produktkultur* (Bonn, 1998).

23   Cf. Gert Selle and Jutta Boehe, *Leben mit den schönen Dingen* (loc.cit.); Gert Selle, *Siebensachen. Ein Buch über die Dinge* (Frankfurt, 1997).

24   Cf. Bazon Brock, 'Zur Archäologie des Alltags', in *Das gewöhnliche Design. Dokumentation einer Ausstellung des Fachbereichs Gestaltung der Fachhochschule Darmstadt* 1976, Friedrich Friedl and Gerd Ohlhauser (Cologne, 1979).

25   Ibid.

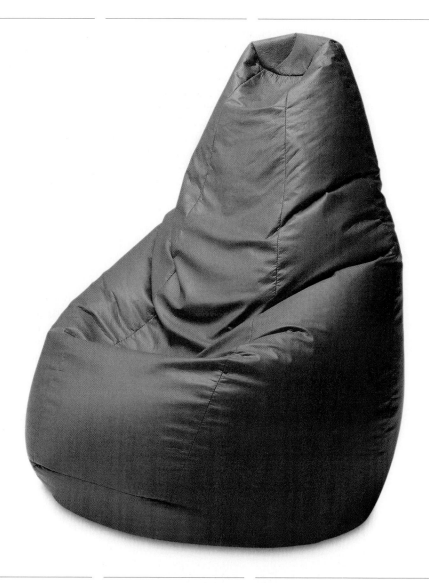

Pierre Gatti, Cesare Paolini, Franco Teodoro, "Sacco", Zanotta, 1968/69

The "Sacco" seating object, for instance, was seen as a prototype of "Antidesign", since it explicitly allows for freedom of use, supports various forms of sitting and – especially among young people – became a symbol for a cool way of "hanging about", which simultaneously symbolised a critical position towards encrusted social structures. This high degree of freedom of use is interesting in the context of NID, even if the sitting convenience is somewhat neglected.

[Cf. Koening, Giovanni Klaus: 'Tertium non datur, 1983', in: *Möbel aus Italien. Produktion Technik Modernität*, no place, no date]

science that deals with the documentation and analysis of art and culture; the culture of the everyday, however, is ignored apart from a few exceptions.[26] Boehncke and Bergmann agree[27] that in general cultural history there seems to be no place for our everyday things. You will search in vain for a reference to the paper clip – this small object that so cleverly enables flexible structures at work – not just in *The Encyclopedia Americana*[28] but also in *La grande encyclopédie Larousse*[29], in the *Brockhaus Enzyklopädie*[30] and *Meyers enzyklopädisches Lexikon*[31].

Panati's *Universalgeschichte der Dinge*[32] or Boehncke and Bergmann's *Die Galerie der kleinen Dinge*[33] are two examples for more recent writing on an exemplary history of objects. However, these studies focus more strongly on the historical, cultural and sociological aspects of changes in use than on utilisation for purposes other than the one originally intended.

Although we could observe an increased interest in the world of objects throughout the last few years, where things have become the lead actors endowed with cultural character – see for example Sack's *Alltagssachen*[34] or Cornfeld and Edward's *Quintessenz*[35] –, the relevant papers, especially those that deal with usage redefinitions, simply provide anecdotal evidence of using the things around us for purposes other than those they were intended for. There is no awareness of the potential and the consequences that are implicit in these forms of appropriation. In trying to create records of the history of the everyday, the enthusiasm of private collectors can be helpful: In his exhibition "MAN transFORMS"[36] Hans Hollein, for instance, presented the cultural history of the hammer – one of our simplest and oldest tools, which has undergone a continuous redesign due to changing applications. The concept of the hammer has been transferred to new areas, resulting in a variety of forms such as the sledgehammer and the surgeon's and astronaut's hammer.

It should be obvious what all these references to redefinitions of use tell us: The phenomenon of NID refers to an innate ability of humankind to develop solutions for situational problems through the use of what is at hand. That the knowledge of those

---

26   Cf. Jacob Burckhardt, *Die Kunst der Betrachtung. Aufsätze und Vorträge* new edition (Cologne, 1997); Norbert Elias, *Über den Prozeß der Zivilisation* (Frankfurt, 1997); Georg Simmel, *Philosophische Kultur. Über das Abenteuer, die Geschlechter und die Krise der Moderne* (Berlin, 1998).

27   Cf. Heiner Boehncke and Klaus Bergmann, *Die Galerie der kleinen Dinge. Ein ABC mit 77 kurzen Kulturgeschichten alltäglicher Gegenstände vom Aschenbecher bis zum Zündholz* (Zurich, 1987).

28   Cf. *The Encyclopedia Americana* (Danbury 1985).

29   Cf. Mémo Larousse. *Encyclopédie générale, visuelle et thématique* (Paris, 1990).

30   Cf. *Brockhaus Enzyklopädie* (Mannheim, 1986).

31   Cf. *Meyers enzyklopädisches Lexikon* (Mannheim, 1971).

32   Cf. Charles Panati, *Universalgeschichte der ganz gewöhnlichen Dinge* (Frankfurt, 1994).

33   Cf. Heiner Boehncke and Klaus Bergmann, *Die Galerie der kleinen Dinge* (loc.cit.).

34   Cf. Manfred Sack, *Alltagssachen. Eine Sammlung von allerlei notwendigen Gebrauchsgegenständen* (Vienna, 1992).

35   Cf. Betty Cornfeld and Owen Edwards, *Quintessenz. Die schönen Dinge des Lebens* (Munich, 1987).

36   Cf. Hans Hollein, *Design. MAN transFORMS. Konzepte einer Ausstellung* (Vienna, 1989).

instances of NID is inherent in our general culture and that it accompanies us from childhood is borne out, on the one hand, by the fundamental examples we can find in cultural history: according to Elias[37], the French aristocracy used forks not only for eating but also to scratch their heads under their wigs. On the other hand, we can list arbitrary examples and text references from our everyday life as evidence for this phenomenon: Just because we know these situations so very well, we tend to smile when Sack[38] tells us about clumsy attempts to open letters using our fingers or knives, or about paper clips being bent into wild works of art when we need something to calm down our nerves. Although there are no studies on this subject, and despite literature touching upon this topic only very rarely, and there being no school to teach us this kind of behaviour, we can assume that this is a specifically human ability that we should come to know and appreciate.

Design Publications

The core issues of design literature have so far mainly dealt with questions of products, their semantics and functionality as well as with the relationship between designed object and designer. Designers are still following the principle that the use of objects has to be determined, or at least suggested, by their design. The idea or intention behind this thinking is usually expressed in terms such as "user-friendliness": the designer becomes the "friend" of the users and wants to help them in understanding and using things in the way they were intended.

The better part of the methodological literature deals with these different approaches – from the functionalist tradition and concepts that also consider emotion, to the neo-baroque styles. The relevant design concepts are introduced in detail, explaining economical and ecological production processes, presenting social concepts of production such as "Universal Design"[39], and documenting marketing strategies for successful product introduction and solutions for ecological disposal. There is only one element in the production chain that is usually neglected: product use. Numerous publications deal with the design diversity of product families (such as chairs, industrial products etc.) but a search for debates as to how and why these products are used in everyday life will yield no results. Objects are presented in glossy photographs with elaborate studio lighting in a sterile environment. The users are as absent as they are in the accompanying descriptions. They reappear, however, reduced to their bodily measurements in ergonomic studies, as for example in a photo series on the use of

---

37   Cf. Norbert Elias, *Über den Prozeß der Zivilisation* (loc.cit.).

38   Cf. Manfred Sack, *Alltagssachen. Eine Sammlung von allerlei notwendigen Gebrauchsgegenständen* (Vienna, 1992), p. 68 ff.

39   Cf. Roger Coleman, ed. *Design für die Zukunft. Wohnen und Leben ohne Barrieren* (Cologne, 1997).

the "Frankfurt Kitchen"[40], in which the housewife happily sashays through a rational-ised workspace to fulfil her tasks. Alternatively, users are reduced to their buying power when featuring in market research statistics which do not say anything about what happens to the objects and their users after the act of purchase.

These deficits have been pointed out time and again. As early as the 1980s, and due to the fact that 58 per cent of newly launched products end up as flops, Brigitte Wolf called for scientific research into everyday life to analyse our behaviour in using things and to make the results available for product design.[41] Bazon Brock also criti-cises a concept of design "that is solely concerned with the object and neglects the re-lationship between user and object."[42] Gert Selle adds that "design history largely hap-pens as anonymous designing and using, but is not apprehended [...]."[43] If everyday life is indeed such a treasure trove of continuously performed anonymous design, the ad-ditional question arises as to "why the functional design impetus is implemented most naturally in instances where designers have least interfered"[44] and why this knowledge has not been used.

It is surprising indeed, that, in spite of these questions having been posed as early as the 1980s, there is still no qualitative design research today, or research into every-day life respectively, that analyses design through use. Although the phenomenon we have termed NID has been sporadically identified, and referenced as "an outright hu-man ability" by Flusser,[45] no-one has, so far, given it more consideration than a passing reference.

40 The Frankfurt Kitchen, designed in 1925 by Grete Schütte-Lihotzky, enabled rationalised housework in the smallest space. Based on the cramped living conditions of the new workers' estates in the 1920s and due to its strict, systematic arrangement, the kitchen is rather reminiscent of a laboratory and is generally regarded as the predecessor of the fitted kitched. See also Grete Lihotzky, 'Rationalisierung im Haushalt', in Das neue Frankfurt I (Frankfurt, 1926/27); Bruno Taut, Die neue Wohnung. Die Frau als Schöpferin (Leipzig, 1924); Gert Selle, Geschichte des Design in Deutschland (Frankfurt, New York, 1994); ed. Deutsche Verlagsanstalt, Geschichte des Wohnens 1918–1945 – Reform, Reaktion, Zerstörung (Stuttgart, 1996).

41 Cf. Brigitte Wolf, Design für den Alltag (loc.cit.), p. 100.

42 Bazon Brock, 'Zur Archäologie des Alltags', in Das gewöhnliche Design, Friedrich Friedl and Gerd Ohlhauser (loc. cit.), p.24.

43 Gert Selle, Siebensachen. Ein Buch über die Dinge (loc.cit.), p. 205.

44 Friedrich Friedl and Gerd Ohlhauser, Das gewöhnliche Design (loc.cit.), p.11.

45 Vilém Flusser, Dinge und Undinge. Phänomelogische Skizzen (Munich, 1993), p. 17.

Use and Usefulness in Sociology

Much of sociology is concerned with studying how consumers use designed objects, an interest that is shared with market research. In order to attain insight into behaviours related to object use, a number of comprehensive studies were developed. The concept of "social setting" (developed in the 1980s by the Heidelberg Sinus-Institute)[46] divides the population of Germany into eight groups exhibiting different lifestyles. The categorisation is closely linked to the income levels of the respective groups. There is, for example, the "petit bourgeois milieu", "which is made up of old age pensioners, lower-level employees and self-employed individuals with a low to mid-level income", or the "technocratic-liberal milieu", which is characterised by high or extremely high income levels."[47] The researchers found that particularly in those groups with higher incomes, the utilisation of objects around them started to become less defined. Additionally, the so-called "alternative milieu", which is assigned to the higher middle classes, appreciated – and still does today – DIY and second-hand products, in particular in the context of sustainability and ecological awareness. Directly opposed was the "non-traditional workers milieu", originating from the "lower classes", which used the world of objects to keep up with the middle classes. (Today, however, the lower and middle classes are more often in competition regarding the opposite "precariate affiliation".) The "hedonistic milieu" forms an exception; it includes members from almost all social strata (except for the higher middle and upper classes) and places a great deal of value on "originality and experimentation".[48] These studies show that through identification with particular objects, people reveal themselves as members of a particular group (today we speak of communities) and distance themselves from other groups.

Although the subject of usage re-definition is touched on in this study, its main focus is the purchasing behaviour of the observed groups.

The "generalist" Bazon Brock is also interested in the relationship between humans and objects. In the third part of his work biography[49] his main concern is to make us realise that we have to develop an awareness for the consumer's world we live in. To a large extent, his analysis focuses on the area of the home. In the context of NID, his thesis that it is not only the user who controls the objects but also the objects that influence the behaviour of their users, is of particular interest. However, the question as to what kinds of behaviours are initiated remains unanswered.

---

46   Cf. HdK Berlin, ed. *Objektalltag – Alltagsobjekte, Gestaltungsanalyse, Soziokultur, Geschichte* (Berlin, 1988).

47   Cf. Carlo Michael Sommer, 'Der Lauf der Dinge. Aus der Sozialpsychologie der Alltagsobjekte', in *Daidalos* 40/1991, p. 96 ff.

48   Ibid., p. 96 ff.

49   Cf. Bazon Brock, 'Objektwelt und die Möglichkeit subjektiven Lebens: Begriff und Konzept des Sozio-Design', in *Ästhetik als Vermittlung*, Bazon Brock (Cologne, 1977).

The different observations from the areas of sociology, ethnology, design and psychology (among others: Baudrillard[50], Elias[51], Breidenbach and Zukrigl[52] , Selle[53] , Jonas[54], Heubach[55], Schönhammer[56]) point to the same result, wich is that the function of objects reaches beyond their mere purpose and has a psychological dimension: to represent or to mirror the identity of their owners. The phenomenon of making an object one's own is also part of this wider subject. By endowing objects with meaning that reaches beyond their pure purpose, people take possession of them and provide them with emotional qualities.

And, finally, for Baudrillard the term "symbol" plays a key role: Objects symbolise the body, they are experienced in an anthropomorphic sense and thus allow the subjects a limitless identification.[57]

---

50   Cf. Jean Baudrillard, *Das System der Dinge* (loc.cit.).

51   Cf. Norbert Elias, *Über den Prozeß der Zivilisation* (loc.cit.).

52   Joana Breidenbach and Ina Zukrigl, *Tanz der Kulturen. Kulturelle Identität in einer globalisierten Welt* (Munich, 1998).

53   Cf. Gert Selle and Jutta Boehe, *Leben mit den schönen Dingen* (loc.cit.).

54   Cf. Wolfgang Jonas, *Design – System – Theorie* (Essen, 1994).

55   Cf. Friedrich W. Heubach, *Das bedingte Leben. Theorie der psycho-logischen Gegenständlichkeit der Dinge* (Munich, 1996).

56   Cf. Rainer Schönhammer, 'Vom Umgang mit den Dingen', in *Objekt und Prozess. 17. Designwissenschaftliches Kolloquium Burg Giebichenstein* (Halle, 1997).

57   Cf. Jean Baudrillard, *Das System der Dinge* (loc.cit.).

Related Strategies of Discovery

Art and Literature

Particularly in the 1920s as well as in the 1950s and 60s, literature, fine art and music discovered everyday empiricism as a source of inspiration and as material for aesthetic production. Waste, things that were lying about or found, everyday language and sounds, as well as trivial objects were taken out of their generic, familiar contexts and integrated into works of art. As much as the social conditions and the related art movements might have differed from each other, they shared a common goal: to bring life and art closer together, or, ideally, to amalgamate them. Everyday objects and materials used could be united under the topos of *objets trouvés*.

In his "Merzkunst", his specific form of Dadaism, Kurt Schwitters, for instance, collected tram tickets, labels, ripped-out pieces of newspapers and adverts, tins, cardboard and so on in order to preserve them in images, reliefs, sculptures or stage designs. "The work of art is created by means of a devaluation of its elements. [...] The material is as unimportant as myself. What is essential is shaping it. Because the material is nonessential, I will use any kind of material if the image calls for it. In matching different materials with each other, I have an advantage over pure oil painting since – in addition to setting colour against colour, line against line, form against form etc. – I also evaluate material against material, for example, wood against sackcloth. I call the worldview, from which this kind of art has emerged, 'Merz'".[58]

Marcel Duchamp's ready-mades radically shattered the prevalent concept of art. In 1917, he submitted a urinal, which he had bought at "Mott Works", a company for sanitary installations, to the New York exhibition of the Society of Independent Artists. He signed it using the pseudonym "R.Mutt" and dated it 1917. An outraged jury rejected his contribution. Today the urinal, several copies of which were reconstructed in 1960, has long become a precious museum relic.

While Schwitters stated the equality or indifference of materials and thus integrated the mundane into art, Duchamp chose the opposite way: He took an everyday object without giving it any artistic treatment whatsoever and changed its meaning by changing its context. By placing a trivial object such as a urinal into a space established as, and elevated to, a museum, he proclaimed it art. "The main issue was challenging artistic behaviour the way it was commonly understood. It was about the absurdity of traditional techniques, of traditional ideas in general [...]."[59]

What Moderings, with reference to Marcel Duchamp, characterises as "an indiscriminate amalgamation of all that exists, [...] a confusion of thinking through a disintegration of all fixed definitions of language (word play), of things (ready-mades), of images (*The Large Glass*)"[60], can be found again in the works of the Décollagists from the 1950s onwards. Here, it is billboards and advertising columns that are being "décollaged". "Holistic" advertising messages from everyday life reappear as debased fragments in an artistic context by ripping the paper they are printed on; they become

---

58   Kurt Schwitters, 'Merz', in: *Ararat*, 19, December 1920.

59   Quoted in: Herbert Moderings, *Marcel Duchamp* (Frankfurt, 1983), p. 99.

60   Ibid, p. 98.

images, which are perceived as symbols, without anything having been added to them. On the contrary: they have lost some parts. Just as construction is being deconstructed in some academic discourses, Décollage has deconstructed the collage of the 1920s. Back then fragmented parts from disparate contexts were assembled into a new, if contradictory, whole. The décollages of Raymond Hains, Jacques Villeglé or Mimmo Rotella, on the other hand, disassemble the whole.

Out of all the numerous literary works that demolished traditional grammar, destroyed established meanings and significations, that integrated dialect and coarse slang into poetry, we might just cite the "list poems" of the 1960s Concrete Poetry as an example. Just as in fine art, series taken from everyday life in the form of word chains were turned into poetry through declaring them as such and putting them into the respective written form. Those could be lists taken from telephone directories, copies of shopping lists, content inventories or the like.

In experimental music, composers and artists have incorporated noise and ambient sounds into their works, have let chance (which, in fact, follows mathematical rules) and thus time govern the succession of sounds and silence, or have turned the sounds we create through the use of objects rather than instruments into music. John Cage, Mauricio Kagel, and La Monte Young could be named as representatives of these movements.

Architecture

As opposed to the aforementioned areas, there seem to be no connections between architecture and its strategies and constructions on the one hand, and the Non-Intentional Design project on the other. With its clearly defined purpose, its complex technical specifications and its dimensions, the construction of buildings rules out any ideas of found objects, intuition, everyday material and so forth. Architecture in the sense of the construction of buildings is always an expression of a preconceived, highly complex and purpose-oriented design. Exceptions like those collected in Bernard Rudofsky's famous publication[61] with the telling title *Architecture without Architects* usually focus on cultures from eras before modernism and can therefore not be considered within the framework of this project. Other examples where laypeople obsessively created bizarre houses (see, for instance, the "Watts Tower" built from thousands of bottles) are also irrelevant since, in these cases, there was an explicit design intention, a plan to create a particular construction.

So in conclusion we can state that architecture and its processes are not suited to defining the field of NID. However, we need to analyse carefully to what extent the use of interior and exterior spaces for purposes other than they were intended for might fulfil the categorical definitions of NID: if, for example, an old bunker is used as a party

---

61   Cf. Bernard Rudofsky, *Architecture without Architects. A short introduction to non pedigreed architecture* (New York, 1964).

venue by young people, if techno-parties take place under bridges, or if former play-rooms are turned into workshops or utility rooms after the children have left home. These spatial redefinitions present borderline cases since we can assume that many of them are rooted in a more or less conscious will to re-design.

The same is true for socially problematic conditions where homeless people try to secure themselves some form of home, private space or somewhere to sleep through the use of means other than architectural materials and construction: although using cardboard boxes as furniture underneath a porch, in a wall recess or under a bridge does conform to the conditions from which instances of NID arise – that is an acute case of emergency or need – the background here is indeed a social deficit and hence these examples represent another NID borderline case.

Science

The history of science is abundant with examples of unusual strategies of discovery, surprising intentions, "un-scientific" methods for the understanding of natural phe-nomena or the discovery of rules, laws and theories. Under closer scrutiny it becomes clear that strategies of discovery, and in particular forms of explanation and represen-tation, are not guided solely by a rational, scientific interest. Human perception of real-ity is based on a curious tension between sensual perception, impressions of the exte-rior appearance of a given situation, and ideas, inner representations, imaginations and projections, through which familiar patterns of thinking are broken up. In the his-tory of science, intuition, epiphany, "aisthesis", but also aesthetics and elegance play a rather substantial role in the realisation, discovery and formulation of rules and evi-dence. In 1725, for instance, Scottish philosopher Francis Hutcheson explicitly spoke about the "beauty of theorems".[62]

From the wealth of material documenting instances of unconventional, almost illogical, moments of insight[63], just one anecdote about Danish physicist Niels Bohr should serve as an example. One evening during a skiing holiday with some scientist friends, he was doing the washing up when he reportedly shouted: "Now I know how science works! It's like washing up. Here in the sink I have dirty crockery, which is swimming in dirty water and treated with a dirty cloth. Still, all the plates and cups are clean afterwards. In science, I also start with unclear ideas, which I test in unclear experiments, the results of which I interpret using an unclear language and its inscru-table grammar. Nonetheless, at the end of the exercise I know that I know a bit more than before."[64]

---

62   Cf. Francis Hutcheson, *An Inquiry Concerning Beauty, Order, Harmony, Design* (The Hague, 1973).

63   Cf. Subrahmanyan Chandrasekhar, *Truth and Beauty* (Chicago, 1987); D.W. Curtin, ed., *The Aesthetic Dimen-sion of Science* (New York,); Ingo Rentschler, Barbara Herzberger, and David Epstein, ed., *Beauty and the Brain* (Basle, 1988).

64   Quoted in: Ernst Peter Fischer, *Das Schöne und das Biest* (Munich, 1997), p. 140.

What can be learned from this type of approach in science is a fundamental, inquisitive openness towards all that might be encountered, even if it happens in an unexpected and unplanned manner and outside of any strict, experimental trials or mathematical calculations.

Intentional Re-Design

Before introducing actual instances of NID, we will – in this chapter – consider situations where objects are used differently from their intended purpose, but cannot be regarded as actual cases of NID according to our definition. At this point it seems useful to restate our understanding of the term: NID denotes a re-purposing of objects due to a situational need. The intentions behind these cases of re-purposing are neither couched in a context of design or art nor in a commercial one. An enforced or conscious renouncement of particular products is also based on different motivations. The parallels and differences described here shall serve to demonstrate that NID is located in an environment related to intentional redesign, a careful analysis of which could, at a future date, be the subject of an interesting follow-up to this publication.

Design as a Manifesto

Throughout the last 50 or so years, re-definitions of use in professional design have taken place against various backgrounds. The method of associative design was developed in Italy.[65] As early as the Bel Design era – the name used by Italian product design during the 1950s and 60s to describe its work, similar to the German approach of *Die Gute Form* –, the Castiglioni brothers started to integrate re-definitions of context and use into their products by referring to already existing principles. This approach mirrored their playful design methods and the brothers managed to win over the market with their new ideas: Today, many of their products have become design classics such as, for example, two stools from 1957, for which the Castiglionis used a tractor and a bicycle seat respectively.

With *Disegno radicale* from the 1960s Pop era, design disassociated itself for the first time from the interests of the manufacturers and and embraced political goals. Not just through products, but also through statements and publications, the radical design movement sought a critical discourse with the capitalist consumer society. It propagated a design that was more closely linked to people's needs, was meant to develop concrete solutions and that also increasingly involved the supply of services. Simultaneously, the new "Antidesign" movement was brought to the attention of the public.[66]

To this end design groups such as "Superstudio"[67], "Archizoom", "UFO", "999" and "Strum" were formed whose concepts broke fresh ground and laid the foundations for an intellectual discourse in design.

---

65   Cf. Alfonso Grassi and Anty Pansera, *Atlante del Design Italiano 1940–1980* (Milan, 1980); Vittorio Gregotti, *Il disegno del prodotto industriale. Italia 1860–1980* (Milan, 1982).

66   Cf. François Burckhardt, *Design als Postulat am Beispiel Italiens* (Berlin, 1973).

67   Cf. Gianni Pettena, *Superstudio. 1966–1982. Storie, figure, architettura* (Florence, 1985).

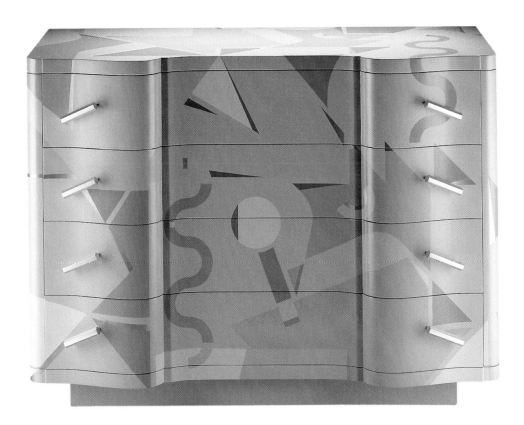

Alessandro Mendini, "Cetonia", Zanotta, 1984

After its "radical" ideas, in the late 1970s and early 1980s, the "Alchimia" group undertook a re-appraisal of everyday objects. With his paint finishes the designer Alessandro Mendini transformed discarded household items into contemporary design objects.

[Cf: Sato, Kazuko: *Alchimia*, Berlin 1988]

Italian Provocations

As early as the 1950s, the brothers Achille and Pier Giacomo Castiglioni designed furniture that was constructed using different parts of various industrial products. For them design implied new combinations of, and new ways of using, existing things, thus endowing each of their products with an individual object character. When asked how they arrived at these principles, they said that everything had already been there, they hadn't designed anything.

[Cf. Giovanni Klaus Koening: 'Tertium non datur, 1983', loc.cit.]

2

3

nille and Pier Giacomo Castiglioni, Zanotta:
'Toio", lamp with car headlight, 1962
'Sella", stool with bicycle saddle, 1957
'Mezzadro", stool with tractor seat, 1957

Even in contemporary design practical and ironic repurposing of everyday objects can be found.

1

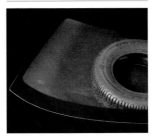

2

3

4

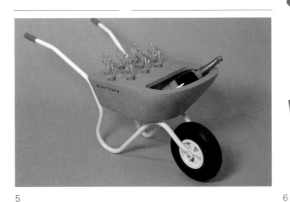

5

6

1-3 Wyssem and Cécile Nochi, limited-edition, in-house production, c/wn_product made in Lebanon, 2006:

1 "Naïve Waterbed in 1/4", sofa with water bottles

2 "Goodyear® riot shopping", coffee table with car tyres

3 "Anticipation no explosive", table with street sign and "Holcim@ultralight concrete ideas", sofa made from cement sacks

4 Isabel Hamm, "Flying Saucer", serving dish, DIM, 2003

5 Alexis Georgacopoulos, "Garden Party" bottle cooler-wheelbarrow, prototype for Veuve-Clicquot, 2007

6 Volker Albus, "Fritz", child's bed tray, prototype for Nils Holger Moormann, 2004

In the second half of the 1970s this was followed by the design group "Alchimia"[68] who used their mundane designs to proclaim trivial culture as the new high culture.[69] Alessandro Mendini, the brains behind this style, implemented this approach through the concept of decorating old pieces of furniture and through re-interpretations of design classics by adorning them with paintings, ornaments, baubles and flags.

At the beginning of the 1980s these movements had reached their zenith. They came to an end with the foundation of the "Memphis"[70] group. The new concepts from Italian design, which were presented in all their various forms, from Bel Air to Alchimia, in the 1972 *New Domestic Landscape*[71] exhibition in the Museum of Modern Art in New York, had initiated an international re-orientation in design and eventually ejected the doctrine of functionalism. These new design approaches were only made possible through close collaboration with craft businesses and small to medium-sized manufacturers who produced the new designs in small series. A more intensified use of media and marketing strategies further contributed to establishing these new groups in the public mind.

In the 1980s, an independent German counterpart to the Italian movements started to emerge, setting itself apart both from the German tradition of "good form" and from the idea of functionalism, which had been perpetuated by the teachings of the Bauhaus and the Ulm School. Exhibitions such as *Gefühlscollagen – Wohnen von Sinnen* in Düsseldorf and the gallery "Möbel Perdu" provided a public platform for the New German Design, which it used for instigating a public debate through its alternative methods. The "New German Design" from the 1980s used all kinds of everyday objects from areas other than the domestic sphere and transformed them into furniture. "After my master craftsman examination I wanted to get away from all these carefully planned actions and for two or three years, together with the sculptor Ulrike Holthöfer, I constructed furniture in a more spontaneous way, mainly using found objects. We were inspired by things that were lying around and which we combined to create interior items and objects."[72] Objects made from trivial everyday materials were created in small series, or as one-off pieces: the "Consumer's Rest Chair" by "Stiletto", for instance, where a shopping trolley was redesigned into a TV chair, or other designs that integrated alleged waste products from the consumer society – an approach implemented in particular by the group "des-in" with, for example, their 1977 "Reifensofa" made from used car tyres.

Design groups like "Bellefast", "Kunstflug", "Ginbande", "Stiletto", or "Pentagon" represented the new confidence of design and its conceptual standards, the main goal of which was not to manufacture industrial products but to provide a critical examination of consumer society. The products were first of all used as statements or, to quote

---

68   Cf. Kazuko Sato, *Alchimia* (Berlin, 1988).

69   Cf. Bernhard E. Bürdek, *Geschichte, Theorie und Praxis der Produktgestaltung* (Cologne, 1991).

70   Cf. Barbara Radice, *Memphis Design. Gesicht und Geschichte eines neuen Stils* (Munich, 1988).

71   Cf. Museum of Modern Art, Italy – The New Domestic Landscape (New York, 1972).

72   Axel Kufus, 'Material und Arbeit', in *Kamingespräche. Designerinterviews und -monologe*, Andreas Brandolini (Kassel, 1994).

Designer's Block, Fuori Salone, Milano 2008

The products of many young designers are inspired by pre-existing objects.

1

2

3

4

5

6

7

8

1–3   Glasgow Caledonian University, Department of Product Design:
1   Gordon Podmore, "Bicycle chair", stool with saddle, pedals and car tyres
2   Colin Bruce, "Pipe dreams", stool from heating pipes
3   Fred Birse, "Soft drinks (number 257)", seat made from empty drink bags
4   Daniela Pais, "Phil", bag for sewing leftovers in the shape of a soft toy
5   Marcella Foschi, "Cassette Wallets", wallet with music tapes
6   Mattia Frongia, "Handl Eggs with care", lamp with egg and packaging
7   Zpstudio, "Windy", lamp with sink plunger
8   Marcella Foschi, "Dressing Lamps", wearable lamps

the magic Italian word, as *progetto*. This also included attempts to use confusion and caricature, unusual materials and suggestions for new ways of using things in order to create awareness of the fact that designed objects are all but natural, self-evident, and logical, and thus to try and communicate new experiences with, and perceptions of, these objects.[73]

When design eventually arrived in the galleries and museums, it revealed a – for Germany – unprecedented proximity to the arts, which, in 1987, resulted in an invitation to the most internationally renowned art exhibition documenta. Like the artists before them, who had used the treasure trove of everyday objects for their work, designers too began to refer to already existing things and changed or modified them in order to create new concepts of use and new sensual experiences. Inititated through the design movements of the 1980s, this marked the beginning of conceptual design in Germany, which – through its social implications – also led to an analysis of living, working and domestic culture.

In her essay "Wo bleibt der Designer? Über Identität und Pluralität" (Where is the Designer? On Identity and Plurality)[74] Gudrun Scholz presented a range of examples demonstrating the main intentions of New Design in Italy and Germany. Some of these approaches are also relevant in the context of NID: Scholz referred to the new use of waste objects as "context transfer". The "radicalisation of everyday life" was predominantly related to materials. In this context, "radicalisation" did not mean "trivialisation" but rather had to be understood as taking everyday life seriously in the sense that the repertoire of everyday materials was used in an uncompromising way. The term "CutUp" described new combinations of materials and collages of things, which could also include historic elements. And finally there was the construction of "hybrids", in which, contrary to the traditional concept of homogeneity in design, trivial objects were changed through the addition of extrinsic elements.

Even if the intention was different to that of NID, these approaches displayed the same associative ability: both in terms of using existing products and by combining them in new ways with the aim of positioning them in new contexts of meaning and use. Due to their role as social statements, however, the usability of these new products took a back seat.

Scarcity Societies

Large scale re-use of existing objects can be observed in societies that – according to western consumerist standards – are seen as non-developed, or during times when the majority of the population experiences a shortage of products or materials. In this context, we will elaborate on the following three examples: firstly the GDR, secondly

---

73   Cf. Uta Brandes, *Design ist keine Kunst. Kulturelle und technologische Implikationen der Formgebung* (Regensburg, 1998).

74   Gudrun Scholz, 'Wo bleibt der Designer? Über Identität und Pluralität', loc.cit.

the periods after the two world wars in Germany, and thirdly the so-called third world countries. Although the particular reasons for, and the extent of, poverty in those societies are or were very different, we will focus on the aspect of work as a significant common factor: After the world wars, the German population, and since 1949 also that of the newly-founded GDR, was suffering from poverty.[75] This is all the more true today for the non-developed countries.

German Democratic Republic (GDR): Instructions for DIY

Depending on how many objects and materials are available, collective patterns of re-definitions of use emerge which are practised by so many people that the "wrong" use becomes the commonly accepted, and thus the right one. Apart from personal and individual inventions, there were even magazines in the GDR that provided tips on how to produce things that were lacking by using those that were available. The East German *Guter Rat für Haus und Kleid* (Good Advice on Housing and Dressing) was set up immediately after the war, when, in November 1945, the Soviet military administration issued a printing permit to a small Leipzig publishing house. The magazine provided patterns for children's clothing made from uniforms, manuals for the construction of "Kochkisten" (cooking boxes), but also introduced new consumer goods and printed manuals for constructing them at home.[76]

The transition from a situation of scarcity brought about by war to one created by a state-directed economy was also documented in the magazines: in 1967 the first issue of *practic*[77] was published. It was based on its 1958 predecessor *Modellbau und Basteln* (Model Building and Crafts), the main focus of which had been the provision of instructions for making models of military or other machinery. *practic*, on the other hand, was aimed at providing advice on the modification and rebuilding of everyday objects. The magazine's success was based on its close cooperation with its readers who contributed their own suggestions and ideas. There was, for instance, a variety of proposals for building a salon-type hair-drying. One reader submitted his invention, which consisted of a tripod, a plastic bag, a hand-held hair dryer and a rubber ring. A few years later another reader introduced a further development of this model: In order to solve the problem that the "traditional" plastic bag version would only dry the superficial layers of hair, he had added a plastic bucket to guarantee a better distribution of hot air. Further interesting examples included a hand-held mixer made from an electric shaver, aluminium baking tins used as reflectors, a ventilator made from a tea infuser, or a bedside lamp for children, which could be constructed using a rubber duck and a soap dish. But also construction manuals for complex electrical and electronic prod-

---

75 This has to be differentiated for the former GDR: From the 1960s onwards there was no existential poverty any more but a lack in product variety, or a lack of specific product groups and materials respectively.

76 Cf. Dominique Krössin, 'Wie mache ich's mir selbst?', in *Wunderwirtschaft. DDR-Konsumkultur in den sechziger Jahren*, ed. Neue Gesellschaft für Bildende Kunst (Cologne, Weimar, Vienna, 1996), p. 160–165.

77 Ibid. p. 161 ff.

ucts such as radios, mini tape recorders, audio-mixing consoles and remote control transmitters were submitted. The primary motivation for the GDR DIY enthusiasts was – besides the joy of spending their spare time doing handicrafts – the desire to solve a situation of acute scarcity in functional and practical consumer goods.

"The trigger for the huge interest in handicrafts in the GDR was rooted in a deficiency and shortfall of supply, in sloppily produced and dysfunctional products. The hobbyists helped out where there had been a lack of motivation or energy in the production process. They provided makeshift solutions for a poorly planned production of consumer goods. Improvisation, the use of substitute materials, or re-using material, as well as making appliances fit-for-purpose – in other words recycling procedures like the ones you would find in any ecological manual – characterised the work of the hobbyists."[78]

The *practic* magazine clearly had a political-ideological agenda as well: the advancement of the "scientific and technological revolution". This idea, however, soon faded into the background and was replaced by the dissemination of pre-industrial craft skills, which are part of the classic body of knowledge for DIY enthusiasts.

Although it is likely that the readers of *practic* used the construction manuals because they were personally confronted with shortages and not so much for ideological reasons, the handicraft activities of the GDR citizens cannot be considered nonintentional. The fact that these changes of use were carried out by following a manual indicates that there were no sudden situations of need from which those re-definitions of use might have arisen. The second reason why we cannot attribute these changes in use to the phenomenon of NID is that scarcity is a constantly present factor in a poor society. Thus the respective solutions are the result of a conscious process; using existing objects differently or reusing them in different contexts is a deliberate act, in which something new is created.

Had there been any readily available products fulfilling the same purposes, this particular kind of inventive hobbyist culture would, in all likelihood, not have existed.

The Post-War Period: Turning Steel Helmets into Chamber Pots

For the same reasons as above we cannot consider the redefinitions of use that happened during the post-war period in West Germany as instances of NID. The general scarcity of everyday goods after the Second World War was limited to a much shorter period of time. In 1989, on the occasion of the 40th anniversary of the foundation of the Federal Republic of Germany, the Werkbund Archive staged an exhibition with the title *Blasse Dinge*[79] (Pale Objects), which collected everyday objects from the years 1945 to 1949. Many of these objects had been produced using wartime materials: candleholders made from gas masks, flower vases built from detonator tins, even a funnel created using a chopped-up bazooka was on show. There were also other objects that had

---

78   Ibid. p. 162.

79   Cf. Werkbund-Archiv, ed., *Blasse Dinge, Werkbund und Waren 1945–1949* (Berlin, 1989).

been constructed by melting and recasting any metal that was left over from military production. Especially aluminium, an expensive material that, due to its low weight, had mainly been used in the production of aeroplanes and engines, was available in abundance after the war and was used for making cooking pots. In his introduction to the exhibition catalogue, Eckhard Siepmann[80] mentions one significant aspect, the ornamental adornment of these objects, which should serve as further indication that these changes of use were very deliberate actions.

These adornments might have been symbols of re-possession: the "beautification" of a formerly menacing object.

The capitalist "Wirtschaftswunder" should soon guarantee a sufficient supply of consumer goods in West Germany, thus, compared to the GDR, putting an early end to the improvisation skills of the West Germans.

"Third World": Recycling the Waste of the Rich

In countries where the population has experienced years or decades of scarcity, or the non-existence of particular goods, products from industrial countries are often turned into objects for everyday use. Examples of this type of usage redefinition were shown in an exhibition featuring the material "rubber"[81]: the reuse of old car tyres.

Special workshops that turn the rubber of car tyres into products for daily use can be found all over Morocco, Haiti, or the Philippines. The products are manufactured using tools and techniques from leather processing. Although being a second-hand material, rubber is not regarded as waste but rather as useful and utilizable. It is available at low cost from car repair shops. The workshops then use it to produce buckets, jugs, bags, and shoes, for example. Since rubber products have often turned out to be more durable and functional than their traditional counterparts, rubber workshops have become a serious competition for traditional professions such as potters, basket makers and craftsmen working with leather. Clay pots used to carry water home from the public well are heavier and more fragile than rubber buckets, and rubber horseshoes give the animals more traction on slippery asphalt roads. However, rubber workshops have not only prevailed over traditional products but also over competition from industrially produced plastic goods. They are even able to charge a much higher price for their products. The concept of considering waste as a resource for reusable raw materials is clearly similar to the concept of NID. Although the authors of the article referred to above emphasize the ecological aspects of reusing rubber, this development does not seem to arise out of ecological awareness nor does it represent a spontaneous act. Instead, we are dealing with the technological development of a whole new branch of crafts.

---

80   Cf. Eckhard Siepmann, 'Alltagsgegenstände 1945–1959', in *Blasse Dinge, Werkbund und Waren 1945–1949* (loc.cit.).

81   Cf. Ulrich Giersch and Ulrich Kubisch, 'Das zweite Leben der Gummibereifung. Reifenrecycling durch handwerkliche Umnutzung', in *Gummi. Die elastische Faszination* (Berlin, 1995).

The use of Coca Cola in some countries is another example for a total transfer of function and meaning. In Russia the soft drink is applied to smooth wrinkles, in Haiti it is used in Voodoo ceremonies to bring the dead back to life, and in Mexico Coke is said to help in creating a connection with God. Due to their bellied shape, Coke bottles are seen as symbols of luck on the Japanese Island of South Ryukyu, where they have replaced ceramic figures of pregnant women which used to be placed on altars.[82]

In the context of NID, these examples open up another dimension of usage redefinition: What happens to an object that is taken out of its original cultural context and used in a foreign environment for purposes that seem to be "wrong"? Just as in the case of car tyres, the transformation of western trivial objects into religious symbols in non-European cultures represents a "creative" act and thus has nothing in common with NID. The same is true for the opposite when, for instance, African cult figures are used as jewellery or letter openers.

Ecological Design

The idea of ecological design already emerged at the Bauhaus, the Werkbund and the Ulm School. Following the oil crisis at the beginning of the 1970s, the Club of Rome report was instrumental in promoting the related implications for design by emphasizing their social necessity. The term "Eco-Design" was born, which not only referred to an economic use of raw materials and recycling concepts, but also implicated the sustainability and the multiple use of existing products. Additionally, the media were used to question the attitude towards consumerism in industrial societies. This has become increasingly important in the face of issues such as climate change. The extent of ecological destruction and the urgency of taking over ecological responsibility have meanwhile established themselves in the public mind.

But let us return to the 1970s: With their "recycling design" the group "des-in" did not aim at creating a sales hit when they introduced their sofa made from old car tyres. Instead, they wanted to be provocative and to initiate a change of attitude. On the whole, "avantgarde design" from that period always had an additional ecological agenda: using untreated materials such as steel, rubber and wood saves resources during the production process and encourages imitation. Industrial materials, rusty steel and wooden branches have become socially acceptable and increasingly more people are following Axel Kufus's example of drawing inspiration from things found in scrap yards and re-using them in new ways.[83]

Today, renouncing certain products and the revaluation of already existing solutions are part and parcel of the basic idea of ecological design. As early as 1995, Friedrich Schmidt-Bleek and Ursual Tischner used terms such as "multi-functionality" and "possibilities for multiple and long-term use" when discussing the question of

---

82   Cf. Joana Breidenbach and Ina Zukrigl, *Tanz der Kulturen. Kulturelle Identität in einer globalisierten Welt* (loc.cit.).

83   Axel Kufus, 'Material und Arbeit', in *Kamingespräche. Designerinterviews und -monologe* (loc.cit.), p. 121.

1

2

3

5

Waste as Inspiration

The Berlin-based label "Rafinesse & Tristesse" produces stools and children's kitchens and washbasins out of old olive cans. For them, material that other people would throw away is a source of inspiration. Hand-made, one-off objects are produced, mostly through the use of recycled products (such as tin cans for doll's cooking pans, the lids of tin cans for hob rings, etc.) – which benefits the environment.

In the project A.R.M. (All Recycled Material) the artist Barbara Caveng produces furniture from bulk waste. In so doing, she aims to bring attention to the increasing poverty in our affluent society, and set an example by giving new life to discarded items.

Jörg Jelden, from the Hamburg-based "Trendbüro" calls this new wave of recycling furniture the "Upgrade" society. The motto *aus alt mach neu* (creating new from old) is becoming increasingly relevant, since, after the throw-away society of the 1980s and 90s, people are looking for added value, history and individuality in the products they buy.

[See: Lucia Jay von Seldeneck: "Um-gemöbelt", in *Der Tagesspiegel*, 06 April 2008, http://www.rafinesse-tristesse com, http://www.a-r-m.net.]

Petra Schultz, Karin Yilmaz-Egger and Katrin Gaberell, furniture made from olive cans, Rafinesse & Tristesse, 2006

1/3 "Frizzle Sizzle", children's kitchen hob

2 "Tin Tuffet", stool

Barbara Caveng: E.T.A.T., clothes rack made from upholstered seat frame and discarded wooden boards, A.R.M., 2007

4 Bulk waste as a treasure trove

5 The old upholstered seat

6 The "new" "E.T.A.T." clothes rack

6

"a product's potential to provide usefulness".[84] As an example they cite the safety pin, which mainly serves to create connections between thin materials, but can also be used as a tool to open locks without a key. But not only objects, services, too, can provide usefulness. Various systems of shared use such as leasing and pooling provide flexible options for sharing products between a number of people and thus represent a new exchange economy, in which neighbourly support is used as a currency. Like NID, ecological design is mainly concerned with creating usefulness; initial conditions and intentions, however, are different.

On the other hand NID, due to its very nature, always preserves resources and can thus be considered as an eco-friendly way of acting.

Deliberate Abandonment of Products

Limiting the number of objects around us, however, does not necessarily arise from reasons of ecological awareness or scarcity. A deliberate abandonment of products can also frequently lead to NID solutions. Whether this kind of limitation is rooted in a protest against the consumer society, in an ascetic lifestyle as an expression of religious beliefs, or in a nomadic lifestyle, what all these forms have in common is that the objects surrounding us are carefully selected and can be used in a variety of ways. Mattresses are for sitting, sleeping, resting, and even used as dinner tables. Pots are not only used for cooking but also as a substitute for crockery; they are turned into soup or salad bowls. In this deliberate limitation it becomes obvious how much we are used to having a separate product for each individual function.

As Bazon Brock has pointed out, this attitude is particularly popular among young people: "There are many young people who get by without any furniture; who hang their clothes over a rope, who do not have beds any more but instead use carpeted platforms that also serve as seating areas. And all that not out of mere necessity, but because they don't want it any other way. [...] It is absolutely clear, however, that through emptying the world of objects, the ability to orient oneself is weakened. The first example in this context is that most young people clear out their spaces because they want to get rid of a world of objects, the structure and order of which they cannot yet influence."[85]

The difference to NID in these examples is the deliberate provocation of "NID-rich" situations: Here, the usage redefinitions are an expression of a chosen lifestyle and are communicated as such. While many other instances of NID take place unnoticed, without reflection, or even in a clandestine way (such as using a paper knife to clean your nails), in the deliberate abandonment of products, repurposing is used as a means of demonstrating an individual lifestyle. Nonetheless, this particular ap-

---

84   Cf. Friedrich Schmidt-Bleek and Ursula Tischner, *Produktentwicklung. Nutzen gestalten – Natur schonen, Schriftenreihe des Wirtschaftsförderungsinstituts, vol. 270* (Vienna, 1995).

85   Bazon Brock, *Ästhetik als Vermittlung* (loc.cit.), p. 416.

proach might turn out to be a true treasure trove for NID and might certainly have inspired some commercial designs.

Commercialization

In all major cities you can find design shops that sell products from developing countries.[86] These are original, not intentional, objects that have been commercialized. Interestingly, most of them originate from scarcity societies, or from a context of art or "statement design". Through the transfer into a design shop they have completely lost their connotations of poverty or statement. This might explain why nobody seems to be bothered by the often rather high prices for objects that were created from the leftovers of throwaway societies such as, for instance, baskets made from old cables. What has happened here is a shift in meaning. An object is designed within a situation of acute deficit and the idea is later imported into affluent societies. Now the object no longer serves to eliminate the deficit for which it was originally designed but satisfies a totally different need: authenticity. Whether those objects are indeed imported from the scarcity society of their origin or if they are mass-produced over here does not seem to matter any more.

Other objects, for example, imitate the design of the 1980s. They are not sold as one-off pieces, however, but as *prêt-à-porter*. There is, for instance, a bottle crate which can be turned into a stool through the use of a moulded metal sheet, or a tealight that transforms into a wall-mounted candelabra with the help of a wire construction.

DIYers and Hobbyists

DIYers or hobbyists are people – mostly male – who build, repair or optimise things themselves.

"*Heimwerker* (literally: home worker) was originally the brand name for a tool set consisting of an electric drill and a number of accessories. It was packed in a cardboard box bearing this name. In common language today, the term also refers to the person who uses these tools at home and the verb *heimwerken* (home-working) describes the activity itself."[87]

Is "home-working" a non-intentional activity then? The mere fact that this activity does not only have a special name but has also created a new supply industry for itself, namely the building-supplies market, suggests that a *Heimwerker* is not an NIDer. We will, however, briefly analyse this activity.

---

86   For example: "Handle with Care" and "O.K. Versand".

87   Friedrich W. Heubach, *Das bedingte Leben. Theorie der psycho-logischen Gegenständlichkeit der Dinge* (loc.cit.), p. 141.

In the 1960s, the *Heimwerkers* established themselves as a consumer group in their own right, whose demand for tools, special machines, and materials was soon met by the building-supplies market. Due to a shortage of supply, DIY seems to have played a more significant role in the GDR than in West Germany. The motivation, however, that made people spend time in their workshops was the same in both parts of the country: the recognition achieved through successfully creating or repairing things, and the idea of a self-sufficient lifestyle.

Friedrich W. Heubach has analysed this activity from a psychological point of view and came to the conclusion that the main incentive for the *Heimwerker* was not so much cutting costs or creating useful objects but the actual work itself. During this activity, the *Heimwerker* feels like an active human being who is able to form connections. The products reflect their creators and since they usually remain unfinished, they are left in a state of dependency and represent the individuality of their creators.

Several of the aforementioned aspects support the thesis that DIY cannot be considered an NID activity: the deliberate journey to the building-supplies market in order to buy material, the related feeling of being part of a group, and above all the significance of the psychological implications of this activity, which seem to outweigh the practical ones, identify the *Heimwerker* as a creative and intentional hobby artist.

Strategies of Appropriation

Things cannot be changed and extended only in terms of their materiality but also with respect to their meaning:

In Togo for instance, there is a cult focusing on the water goddess Mami Wata, who is worshipped in the form of a wooden mermaid bearing distinct European features and long straight hair. The figure is dressed in western clothes, wears sunglasses and costume jewellery, and holds a wing mirror in her hand. It is surrounded by powder boxes, perfume bottles, soft drinks, candles, and sweets. Western food is served during festivities in honour of the goddess and people dance to waltz music. This example of integrating western culture and consumer goods into the daily life of a non-European culture is described by the ethnologists Breidenbach and Zukrigl[88] in the context of the question of authenticity in a globalised world.

Although the wooden figure itself has not changed, its meaning has experienced a shift by transferring it into a different cultural context. Sociology and psychology have a special term for this kind of object use: appropriation. Making things your own by endowing them with personal meaning seems to be a deeply ingrained human need.

"If an 'indigenous' man lunges at a watch or a ball pen just because they are 'western' products, we tend to find this absurd or funny because he does not use them at all

---

88   Cf. Joana Breidenbach and Ina Zukrigl, *Tanz der Kulturen. Kulturelle Identität in einer globalisierten Welt* (loc.cit.).

but zealously seizes them in a child-like manner and with an idea of power. Here, the object has no function but a virtue, a characteristic: it becomes a symbol."[89]

Various acts of appropriation can also be observed within the same cultural context. Gifts create a relationship between the giver and the receiver; mementoes and souvenirs form a bridge to the past; lucky charms and talismans have a special power that turns objects into symbols. Every object, especially if it is mass-produced, has to undergo a process of appropriation before it can be truly possessed. The object itself is unaltered by this process and the act of appropriation is rarely a conscious one.

In our context, appropriation has to be considered a central category because it is very close to the implications of NID.

"Thus an object can be used for totally different purposes from those it was intended and designed for. The designer might only be able to give an object some very general characteristics; the user takes over and designs himself in the sense that each use creates, or refers to, often rather self-defined principles of order and interpretation, and dimensions of experience. Behind all the social norms and the appropriate civilisational models of interpreting things lies a vast field of uncountable varieties of individual values, of economies of use and aesthetics of use, which no designer could have ever been, or would ever be, able to imagine; it would only confuse him."[90]

Although Selle and Boehe do not provide us with radically new insights, they articulate something in this quote, which many people – if not even most professional designers – do not seem to be aware of: no matter how hard they think about the potential ways of using their designed objects, whether they give them clever interfaces or provide them with intelligent manuals, the moment the object is sold it is no longer under the designers' control and often also defies their ideas of what happens to it and how it is used. Surprisingly, this does not seem to be of much importance to many designers. Although there are some studies dealing with the use of consumer goods, predominantly in the area of interior design, the focus tends to be on finding sociological conclusions.

A 1986 study by Selle and Boehe provides some insight into this subject:[91] The authors analysed the relationship people form with objects in their homes. Using case studies, they investigated the "behaviours of appropriation" of a particular group of people (middle class, between 40 and 50 years old). They photographed people's homes and held interviews in which the owners explained what kind of things they possess, and why and how they use them. On the basis of three of these case studies, the authors went on to interpret the relevant forms of behaviour. Each object has both a historical and a social aspect. The historical aspect is based on the fact that inherent to things are instructions of use which have been formulated by earlier generations and which are still followed to a large extent. The social component is defined by sticking to norms and rules of behaviour for the use of things that have been established by the society, or

---

89   Jean Baudrillard, *Das System der Dinge* (loc.cit.), p. 106.

90   Gert Selle and Jutta Boehe, *Leben mit den schönen Dingen. Anpassung und Eigensinn im Alltag des Wohnens* (loc.cit.), p. 50.

91   Ibid.

by the social circles, to which people belong. For example, a knife is used at the dinner table for cutting food and not for pricking one's neighbour. Within these guidelines, however, there is some degree of freedom that people make use of. The authors call this "appropriation behaviour" or "obstinacy". There are individual methods of appropriating mass consumer products. Because they are used in a specific, "obstinate", way, things are endowed with additional value for their owners. In their study the authors do not talk about new assignations of function but tend to focus on situations where things are part of family tradition, or have been repaired several times, or through a particular arrangement are endowed with meaning. Selle and Boehe repeatedly emphasise that there is a discrepancy between the ideas designers have about their objects and the actual behaviour of users (and vice versa). They also explicitly point to the fact that design theory so far (1983) had failed to investigate the space between design and use. – This, however, has started to change since this intelligent study was published.

Non-Intentional Design from an Empiricist Perspective

Contradictions in the Object: Design Intention and Use

Form and Function as Characteristics of Use

As an introduction to the visual examples of Non-Intentional Design we will provide a short overview of the relevant design approaches that deal with the object and the implementation of intention in use.

There are two parameters that are constantly mentioned in connection with an object's character: form and function. While function represents an object's "rationality", as it were, and justifies its existence, an object's form embodies its function. The close connection between these two aspects was first signalised by the expression "form follows function". Here, function rules form; it defines the look of an object.

In the context of NID, however, we can observe that similar forms are used for the same purpose even if they were not created to fulfil the same function. We open letters with knives, for instance, and could vice versa use a paper knife to butter bread if we needed to. During such improvised behaviour we are not looking for a function but for a shape that, according to our experience, comes closest to the one which has so far fulfilled the purpose. This reversal of form and function has also been pointed out by Holger van den Boom: "Wittgenstein, however, uses a logical extension of the concept of form: the form of an object represents the possibilities of its appearance in actual situations; its form is the sum of its potential appearances in situations. We have even gone further to state: the form of an object is the sum of its potential appearances in ways of life. [...]

Ergo: the form of an object represents the sum of its potential appearances in situations of use. Therefore we can no longer say: form follows function but rather: form follows use."[92] "Use" makes the user enter into a specific type of object relationship that is located between form and function. The familiar conditions of form and function seem to disintegrate when considering an object's use because, "in principle, we can use everything for anything in a more or less successful way. Contrary to a dedicated function, use is not the entelechy of an object. If something is used for purposes other than those it was intended for, then a purpose different from the one defined by a standardised function has been chosen.[93]

Form does not follow function, but it follows this particular type of use! "[...] Use cannot be planned or firmly designed in a particular sense! The how-to is unrestricted!"[94]

Van den Boom's conclusions hark back to our two initial points of departure, subject and object, which we can use to analyse the phenomenon of NID. "Ways of using

---

92   Holger van den Boom, *Betrifft: Design. Unterwegs zur Designwissenschaft in fünf Gedankengängen* (Braunschweig, 1994), p. 107.

93   Ibid., p. 107 f.

94   Ibid., p. 108 f.

things only exist where there are alternatives. Use implies choice. There is either a particular tool to fulfil an obvious purpose, or there is a defined purpose.

1) different tools for the same purpose: use x (and not y)
2) the same tool for different purposes (multi-functionality): use x
(to achieve z)."[95]

In point one, different solutions arise from an intention, meaning the role of the user is the key. Point two, on the other hand, expresses the potential of the different uses an object has to offer. This differentiation into the perspective of subject and object respectively represents an exciting possibility of further analysis in the area of NID.

Dealing with Meaning

Nowadays semiotics and semantics also play an important role in design.[96] In this context they refer to the ability to interpret intended function and use by looking at an object's shape. Gerda Smets, who teaches theory of form at the Delft University of Technology, adds the aspect of perception to the form-function definition. "According to recent theories of form we do not see shapes but significations of behaviour."[97] In terms of semiotics, it is desirable to achieve an unambiguity of shapes and consequently of the implied significations of behaviour. Effortless identification of things represents the main goal of the semiotic design principle. Any divergence from this rule is experienced as a loss of information. If design intentions are not met and the subject's behaviour deviates from what is expected, this is seen as negative and as something to be avoided. Within this approach, design and designer have failed if objects are not clearly identifiable.

With the advent of new technological products for office and home use in the 1970s, the Offenbach school of design coined the term *Anzeichenfunktion* (indication function). Since the new high-tech products hide their actual functions, design has to create artificial indications that facilitate the identification of purpose and use.

In contrast to these strict design principles, we consider the unambiguity or ambiguity of product semantics as a challenge for design in terms of investigating questions of an open design approach on the one hand, and also as an excellent opportunity to discover multiple ways of use.

Simple objects whose original function is immediately obvious to everyone are best suited for the broad field of re-definitions of use, hence for semiotic and semantic failures. However, we do not experience this characteristic as a confusing or irritating

---

95   Ibid., p. 109.

96   Cf. for example *formdiskurs. Zeitschrift für Design und Theorie*, vol. 3, II/1997. This issue was dedicated to the subject: On language, objects and design.

97   Gerda Smets, 'Neue Experimente zur Wahrnehmung und Gestaltung von Gebrauchsgegenständen', in *Design und Identität*, ed. Norbert Hammer and Birgit Kutschinski-Schuster (loc. cit.) p. 42.

one but instead as an enrichment, in the sense of added value. These instances of in-correct use do not derive from helplessness but from our resourcefulness regarding the use of objects.

If, in the spirit of NID, things are used for purposes other than they were intended for, this is not due to a misinterpretation of their original function, but is instead rooted in our ability to see beyond this and discover abstract or open forms. Nor do we forget the original purpose of an object, so we do not use a knife to open letters because we do not recognise its purpose and interpret letter-opening as its actual function. We use it in such a way because it matches a solution pattern in our head and lends itself to solv-ing a particular problem.

We can assume that knowing the original purpose of an object and understand-ing its function, the clear semiotic instructions, facilitates changes of use because it becomes unlikely that something is involuntarily destroyed through misappropria-tion. It seems that we prefer to avoid the things we do not know. The respect that is usually shown when it comes to high-tech products supports the assumption that, in these cases, proper use is paramount to alternative creative options. This is addition-ally borne out by the strong reservations usually displayed by those not familiar with technology, who tend to feel easily stressed and approach new technologies with ex-treme caution. A high replacement value, and potentially embarrassing situations in which the "abuse", meaning the wrongful use that resulted in destruction, has to be explained, seem to be reason enough for following instructions.[98]

Generally people do not seem to be keen on talking about instances of NID re-lated to changes of use that went wrong. Having to admit that trying to use your mobile phone as a hammer resulted in its destruction does not attest to an independent and clever use of things but rather to stupidity and incompetence. Thus the semiotic ap-proach of communicating function through design alone is not sufficient. Therefore, in addition to a new product we usually receive manuals that are meant to explain its function and use – often in a rather incomprehensible fashion – and that advise us not to use the product for any other purpose than the intended one.

In this context it seems rather paradoxical that a manual by computer manufac-turer Apple recommends the use of a paper clip for solving problems with disk ejec-tion. It is also rather common among camera manufacturers to suggest using a coin to open the battery compartment. The same advice can be found for electric appliances (razors, hair-dryers and so forth) whose voltage can be switched between 220 and 110. And in the case of telephone systems, fax or answering machines, the use of ball pens for pressing minute buttons is almost unavoidable. Although, on the one hand, manu-facturers advise against any non-intentional use of their high tech products, they do not hesitate to recommend the non-intentional use of mundane objects in order to initiate certain functions.

98   The fact that instances of repurposing in the sense of NID can nevertheless be observed in the context of new media will be elaborated in the chapter "New Media".

Everyday Use – Design Intention

The non-intentional use of mundane objects can be observed in almost any area of life. We encounter changes of use at home, in the office, and in public. Once you have started investigating this subject, you will find instances of NID everywhere. In each office you will find the compulsory cup used as storage for pens. In each home there will be at least one chair that is not only used for sitting on, but also as a shelf, clothes rack, or ladder. Is there anyone who has not watered plants using a bottle because there was no watering can at hand? In the streets you will find bicycles locked to lampposts, or with saddles covered in plastic bags to protect them from rain. In front of shops goods are presented on chairs, tables, or cardboard boxes. Tired shoppers take a rest by sitting on steps, or on the edges of plant containers. All this is Non-Intentional Design. In order to give some indication of the enormous spectrum of possible applications of normal, everyday objects, we will show a selection of images from different areas of life which illustrate the prevalence of the phenomenon of NID in our everyday environment.

The images are divided into the three areas of home, work, and the public sphere, and originate from different cultural contexts. The majority of examples, however, come from a European background. As mentioned before, there is a multitude of reasons for using things in ways that differ from their original purpose and one of the most common is poverty. However, these photographs are meant to illustrate that the ability to disassociate things from their original function can be based on a variety of motivations and does not only result from having to make a virtue out of necessity.

The Paper Clip

"
...

A paper clip can be used in all sorts of unintended ways: as a makeshift keyring, as a make-up utensil, for cleaning fingernails or, bent into the right shape, as a small universal tool. Children link up several clips to create bracelets or necklaces. Older children transform the clips into ammunition which they fire off rubber bands which can also be found in an office. [...]

And last but not least, the paper clip is used to calm nerves, comparable to the hand charms used in Oriental cultures. You can find them lying around, distorted and bent into little balls, after tiring business meetings or important telephone conversations.

"
...

Heiner Boehnke and Klaus Bergmann, *Die Galerie der kleinen Dinge. Ein ABC mit 77 kurzen Kulturgeschichten alltäglicher Gegenstände vom Aschenbecher bis zum Zündholz* (Zurich, 1987), p. 34–35.

The Privacy of Home

Home is the space where people can freely express their desires and wants. It is a refuge that provides freedom to fashion it according to one's own preferences, even if economic resources and social milieu tend to impose certain limits on the alleged individuality.

It is also a private space. Undisturbed by any kind of public intrusion, the home-owner can decide who is allowed to enter this space and to which degree. It is a place of relaxation that we use for recovering and spending our spare time in as comfortable and pleasant a way as possible. A typical NID-rich period is the time shortly after having moved into a new home. We know from experience that many of the makeshift solutions created during this time often remain in place for years or even until the next move, be it for reasons of convenience, or because we have come to appreciate these temporary arrangements, or simply got used to them.

Thus we can find two extremes in the same private space: On the one hand, we use this space to express our personality. On the other hand, we feel secure and un-disturbed; we are able to do as we please. Nothing is off limits unless we want it to be. There is no embarrassment. And this is mirrored in the many instances of NID we find in this space.

Within the home, there are again different areas that have to fulfil different purposes. While we usually place more emphasis on functionality in the kitchen and bath-room, the living room is an area for recreation and representation. Therefore we can find different forms of functional changes in those areas. In work areas, like the kitchen for instance, the focus is on rationalising work processes and creating well laid-out and space-saving storage solutions for appliances and foodstuffs.

In the living room, on the other hand, considerations such as aesthetics, repre-sentation, or demonstrating an ideological disposition are of greater importance.

The Kitchen

In the 1980s, industrial furniture and fittings found their way into the private realm. Stainless-steel furniture and industrial goods became accepted in the living room. These new alternatives delighted the design cognoscenti, but they also enjoyed great popularity amongst young people because of their low prices. Items used included aluminium shelving, laboratory glassware, metal food-storage containers, storage hooks and frames, workbench dining tables, cutting mats as cheeseboards and so forth.

3

1 Cellar shelving as kitchen cupboard
2 Aluminium piping as kitchen-roll holder
3 Butcher's hooks for kitchen storage

1

2

3

4

Kitchen utensils and notes

Because of the wide variety of food items and kitchen utensils, need for storage in kitchens is high. Even the smallest nooks and corners are used as storage or hanging space. Sinks and windowsills take on the role of fridge. Also space for day-to-day notes and reminders needs to be found, and the kitchen naturally suggests itself as the obvious place for these "notes-to-self".

7

1 Radiator as kitchen shelf
2 Wine jug as brush holder
3 Planter for storage of flowerpots and trays
4 Flower basket for kitchen rolls
5 Boiler as magnetic board
6 Sink as fridge
7 Sink as waistbin

1

2

3

4

Non-Tainting and Washable

The hygiene characteristics of NIDs in the realm of eating are especially important.

1 Jar as cutlery holder
2 Egg boilers as spice containers
3 Jam jars as spice jars
4 Clothes pegs as bag closures

2

3

The Bathroom

Many instances of repurposing are found in the bathroom that usually begin as temporary solutions, but over time become permanent NIDs. For instance, various types of glass and beaker can be used for toothbrush and paste. Splash-proof surfaces around the toilet, like the cistern, windowsill, radiator or toilet-brush handle are also used differently. Towels get hung to dry over shower-curtain rails, radiators and radiator valve knobs, or on cistern bolts and window handles. In the shower, shampoo and shower gel get placed on the mixer tap or on the edge of the bathtub. Even for the storage of cosmetics, women like to use baskets, flowerpots and jars as holders.

1 Nutella jar for toothbrush and toothpaste
2 Radiator valve as hook
3 Mixer tap as storage for shampoo
4 Radiator as toilet roll holder
5 Toilet brush as toilet roll holder

5

1

2

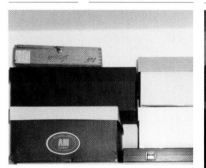

3

4

Storage and Storage Space – Private Recycling

To impose order on the things around us, we need clearly arranged structures. Receptacles and containers of every kind help us to build our own systems of order.

Empty boxes, tins, jars, crates and bags are re-used for various utensils, groceries and articles of clothing. Built-in safes get used as wardrobe space, bookshelves are built from books and planking, a stretched chain becomes a clothes rail.

Particular significance is attributed to the repurposing of packaging. This seems obvious since the earlier purpose of this material was to assemble goods as clearly defined units for sale, to prevent damage to the contents and to keep them clean and fresh.

6

1 Wine crate as holder for office supplies
2 Plastic bags as clothes sacks
3 Cigar- and shoeboxes as holders for loose change, letters, etc.
4 Shoeboxes as drawer dividers
5 Gherkin jar as loose-change holder
6 Rock candy jar as sweet jar
7 Flower pot used for cable storage

1

3

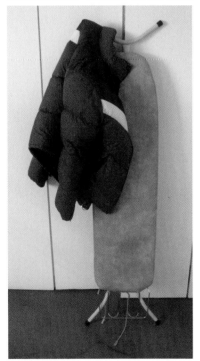

2

4

5

Clothes Hooks – All for One

Taking off and hanging up a jacket or coat is one of the first things done on entering a house. But opportunities for hanging clothes are not only found in the entrance hall. Chairs, mirrors, sofas or even ironing boards can be used to drape clothes over.

The everyday action of hanging up clothes can be fulfilled by many other objects.

Even for wet clothes, there are alternatives to the conventional products: microwaves and radiators can replace the clothes horse; the balcony handrail or a shelf – preferably in the open air – can perform the function of a washing line.

7

1	Ironing board as clothes holder
2	Ironing board as clothes holder
3	Chair as clothes holder
4	Mirror as clothes holder
5	Carpet as hat stand
6	Microwave as clothes dryer
7	Radiator as clothes dryer
8	Balcony handrail as clothes horse
9	Shelf as clothes horse
10	Taps as clothes horse

10

1

3

2

4

1 Chair as clothes rack
2 Chair as clothes rack and shelf
3 Chair as bookshelf
4 Chair as Television table

6

The Chair – One for All

The chair is a prime example of the multiple uses a single object can be put to. Alongside the main seating function, chairs are used for many other and varied purposes. The backrest lends itself particularly to hanging clothes or drying towels, the seat can be used as a step to reach high places and the legs can serve as sporting equipment in gymnastic exercises.

Considering all these instances of repurposing and auxiliary uses, the question arises: how often do we actually use everyday objects in their original design context, and what is the percentage of repurposing? The perception of objects in terms of their multi-functionality confirms the assumption that simple, low complexity objects are extremely suitable for NID.

5 Chair as shelving for toys
6 Chair as night table
7 Chair as night table

1

2

3

4

5

Office Workplace

The workstation is usually the only place in the office where people can exert some personal influence over the design of the space and the order of things. In this otherwise rather impersonal and structured environment, most NID-implementations are to be found on or around the desk. Pencils and other items of stationery are stored in glasses, jars and mugs; monitor screens get co-opted as pin-boards, where post-it notes, postcards and reminders are stuck.

Additionally, there are numerous temporary changes of use, for example, the use of books and pencils as rulers, pencils and scissors substitute for paper knives and paper knives are used to clean fingernails, etc.

8

9

1 Junk mail container used as business-card box, flower pots as pencil holders
2 Table edge as guillotine
3 Clothes line as notice board
4 Clothes line as appointments calendar
5 Cup as pencil holder
6 Monitor as bookend and display shelf
7 Home-made disk box as pencil holder
8 Hardware as letter tray
9 Hardware as paper tray

Public Space

Public streets are spaces of movement but also – in particular in cities – they represent a space for the presentation of goods and for the self-representation of people. In many countries there are considerably more varied means of transport than in Germany, but here too, where we mainly find bicycles and motorcycles in addition to cars, people's desire for change still has enough room for development. Means of transport are used as presentation areas or, in the case of bicycles, are furnished with additional structures that facilitate the transport of goods. In order to prevent theft or provide protection from rain, bicycles are tied to various other immovable objects, or feature plastic bags.

Even in Germany, where we have specific products for each imaginable purpose, shop owners often resort to adapting quite unusual objects for the presentation of their goods: clothes hangers can be found hooked to power cables in front of shops, books are laid out on beer tables or benches, and all sorts of containers are used to store goods which are not usually to be found in them.

It looks like there is either never enough street furniture (public design), or the existing items do not fulfil the desired purpose. During the summer, there are far more people sitting on steps, flower containers, borders, or even on the ground than there are sitting on benches. Flower containers, however, are not only used as seats but also for the presentation of goods, for example by jewellery dealers in pedestrian areas. Lampposts are ideal objects for securing bicycles but also for the application of posters or stickers.

Construction Sites

Change of perspective: while in the private sphere objects and materials from the public realm and from construction sites are transformed into interior items, in the public realm forms are sought that recall well-known household objects.

Here, building materials are employed as a clothes rack, to avoid having to throw clothes on the floor.

1 Building material as helmet stand
2 Reinforcement bars as clothes rack
3 Construction site barriers as clothes rack
4 Shuttering used as shoe storage

2

4

1

2

3

4

5

6

1 House wall as display stand
2 Power cable as clothes rail
3 Beer crate as bottle display
4 Beer table as book display
5 Fork-lift palette as picture-frame display
6 Fruit crate as flower display

8

9

Product Display

When goods are sold outside of retail premises, makeshift solutions are often employed for their presentation.

12

7   Sewing machine as hat stand
8   Fruit basket as party light display
9   Fruit crate as goods display
10   Shoeboxes as presentation stands
11   Pasting table as book display
12   Shoeboxes and basket as
      presentation stands

1

2

3

4

1   Cloth as display for belts and Rubik's
    Cubes
2   Barrier as umbrella stand
3–4 Cardboard box, board and cloth as
    spectacles holder

Markets and Street Vendors

Market stalls are built and taken down again within the space of one day. On the other hand, street vendors, who might trade illegally, often have to have their goods up for sale – and to disappear – within minutes. The required flexibility is achieved through improvising.

6

5 Banana cartons as goods display table
6 Fruit crates as goods display table
7 Banana cartons as display table for toys

1

2

3

4

5

Billposting

The cheaper alternative to commercial advertising hoardings is street furniture, such as wastebins and lampposts in places with a lot of through traffic.

8

1 Shop window as advertising hoarding
2 Letter box as advertising hoarding
3 House wall as advertising hoarding
4 Lamppost as advertising hoarding
5 Lamppost as notice board
6 Window casing as advertising hoarding
7 Building-site fence as advertising hoarding
8 Wastebins as advertising hoarding

1

2

3

4

5

6

7

Sitting

When there is not enough seating in public places, not only young people have ways around the shortage.

1 Steps as seating
2 Monument as seating
3 Straw bales as seating
4 Plant barrier as seating
5 Barrier as seating
6 Barrier as seating
7 Kerbstone as seating
8 Steps as seating
9 Handrail as seating
10 Plinth as seating
11 Temple wall as seating
12 Shop-window ledge as seating

10

12

1

Bars, Pubs and Restaurants

The actual purpose of beer mats is to absorb liquid. Since they usually can be found under each beer glass they are also used for advertising and additionally lend themselves as notepads for the waiting staff.

Some barrels have the same height as tables and serve to indicate the type of restaurant.

1 Beermat as waiter's writing pad
2 Boat as table
3 Barrel as table

2

3

3

4

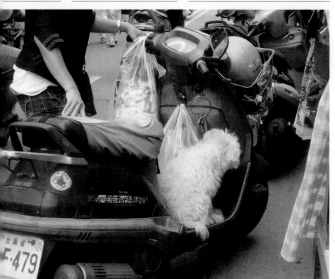

On Two Wheels

Push bikes and motorcycles are practical means of transport in a city, since you can get to your destination quickly, without worrying about parking spaces and traffic jams. The disadvantage is the limited space available for luggage and passengers, so many functional parts are, accordingly, repurposed, often with flagrant disregard for traffic regulations, such as carrying passengers on the crossbar or handlebars – or, as is often seen in Italy, three members of the same family on a scooter with a dog on the running board.

1 Sofa cushions as saddle padding
2 Handlebars used for carrying bags
3 Bag used for canine transport by bike
4 Mailbox used as carrier
5 Vespa used to transport dog

1

2

Mail Delivery

When there are no letter boxes, or the ones that are there are simply inaccessible, the postman will look for suitable alternatives for leaving the post behind securely and visibly. For personal messages, sliding the letter under the door has become the accepted means.

1   Door grille as letterbox
2   Door slit as letterbox
3   Door grille as letterbox

3

Waste Disposal

When there is no wastepaper basket available, the nearest thing that looks like one will do.

1 Bicycle basket as wastepaper basket
2 Bicycle basket as wastepaper basket
3 Newspaper holder as wastepaper basket
4 Shopping trolley as wastepaper basket

3

4

The Personal Computer

" . . . However, the essence of scientific and technological development also entails that knowledge
becomes dispensable. This peculiar characteristic
is rooted, among other things, in the fact that
knowledge is embodied in objects which can not
only be used without access to this knowledge, but
also for purposes totally different from those for
which the objects were originally produced. Think,
for example, of the personal computer which, for
a long time, has been used for purposes other
than computing and without the user having to
understand the embodied knowledge, for example,
about switching circuits. Thus the redefinition of
purpose in the sense of a subsequent discovery of
a new purpose is an intrinsic characteristic of progress. " . . .

Jurgen Renn, *Verehrte An- und Abwesende*, speech on the historical connections
between physics and mass media on the occasion of unveiling a memorial at the
building of the ARD-studio in Berlin, http://www.berlinews.de/archiv/424.shtml
(accessed 16 April 1999).

New Media

"When considering how deeply the computer has penetrated our everyday life, I'm surprised that so far no corresponding design culture has developed, neither in terms of hardware nor software."[99]

New media – this term includes all applications that can be accessed or used via a computer. Here, we will analyse examples of NID emerging in the area of hardware as material manifestations of these new media in our everyday environment, as well as of those arising in the area of software as a virtual dataspace with its own particular structures and rules. The hardware field will be analysed using the example of the personal computer, and our investigation of the digital space will focus on the Internet.

The Personal Computer

In the course of its comparably short existence, the personal computer has amalgamated so many different features that asking for additional, non-intentional ones might seem slightly absurd. Its extensive multi-functionality has given many users a headache and it seems fair to assume that no-one will actually use the complete set of features offered by a PC. However, the amalgamation of the PC with the functions of other high-tech products is constantly progressing: originally developed as a tool, computers nowadays contain the same, or similar, modules as for instance televisions, HiFi systems, or telephones. Hence, it is now possible to use a PC for watching television, listening to the radio or audio CDs, and for making phone calls. The kind of multi-functionality that can be enabled through the complexity of these products has mostly been discovered and developed by users and "freaks". The necessary programmes have usually been distributed in the form of shareware or extensions. The computer and software industry was slow to figure this out.

In 1995, the Israeli company Vocaltec revolutionised the world of telecommunications with their Windows-based programme Internet Phone. All you needed in addition to the software for making international phone calls at local rates was a PC with a soundcard, a microphone, and an Internet connection. Five years later the product was ready to ship and, against strong criticism from the telecommunications industry and from Internet users (who were worried about network overload), was launched onto the market. This was the beginning of VoIP (Voice over Internet Protocol) and all subsequent Internet telephone programmes and services.[100] Thus, with the relevant equipment, many PCs are turned into cheap telephones and increasingly replace the traditional systems in public telephone cafés.

---

99   Boris Müller, student at the Royal College of Art, London, at 'Youngblood Special', speech delivered at 'Profile Intermedia', Bremen, Germany, 6 December 1998.

100   Cf. Detlef Borchers, 'Telefonieren übers Internet wird salonfähig', *Die Zeit*, no. 34 (1996), http://www.zeit.de/1996/34/iphone.txt.19960816.xml 1996.

With headphones, a microphone, internet access, and the appropriate software a computer can become a telephone.

A further example of hardware used for non-intended purposes can be found with the PCs little brother, the Apple iPod. After a five-year history of development, several companies have come up with additional uses for the cult music player that go beyond listening to music: the iPod can be a foreign-language guide, a cookbook, a notebook, a drink or wine lexicon, and even a religious reference tool for either the Bible or the Koran. In connection with a sensor located in a shoe and a wireless adaptor it even becomes a personal trainer communicating relevant data to joggers. These data records can also be saved.[101]

As far as hardware itself is concerned, the relevant literature features a number of technical manuals and design publications. The majority of these publications are concerned with the design of attractive packaging and the integration, or concealment, of the hardware at work or at home. There is, however, little to be found regarding alternative uses.[102] User studies mainly deal with the black-box phenomenon, which provides the designer with a great deal of freedom in designing the exterior appearance of these products. What is interesting in this context is the fact that not the actual functionality, but rather the use, is to be communicated through the design. This, however, is not an easy task since fairly simple actions, such as switching an appliance on or off, hence finding the power switch, can often turn out to be rather nerve-wrecking. Given the multitude of functionality-related problems, it might be understandable that professionals have so far failed to pay due attention to the anarchic field of alternative uses.

The computer manufacturers with their cool, technical products have missed another aspect as well: due to long sessions of use, computer users often develop a close, almost intimate, relationship with their computer. This aspect is in no way captured in the exterior design of PCs. Neglected by industry, a new type of user has emerged: the "modder". Like automobile fans, computer modders use their creative abilities to give their PCs a customised look.[103] They change the dull grey of its exterior by applying jazzy spray-on colours and neon lighting, they replace parts of the casing with glass to provide new insights, fans are equipped with lights, and new patterns are created for the ventilation grilles. Meanwhile, the supply industry has caught on to this trend and provides the relevant products. True modders, however, are always keen on designing their own innovative packaging for their "uncovered" technology. The fancier, the better. CaseCon[104] (case construction) is the name for this new discipline that wraps

---

101 Cf. Gregor Wildermann, 'Intelligente Zweckentfremdungen', *Spiegel Online*, http://www.spiegel.de/netzwelt/tech/0,1518,443726,00.html (accessed 21 October 2006).

102 Except for a number of publications on subversive actions that emerged from new-media groups and that deal less with forms of use than with the description of the issues related to these actions. See, among others, Agentur Bilwet: *Bewegungslehre. Botschaften aus einer autonomen Wirklichkeit* (Berlin, 1991); autonome a.f.r.i.c.a. gruppe, Luther Blisset, and Sonja Brünzels, ed. *Handbuch der Kommunikationsguerilla* (Berlin, 1997); Mark Dery, 'Culture Jamming, Hacking, Slashing and Sniping in the Empire of Signs', in *Open Magazine Pamphlet Series*, 25 (1993).

103 Cf. Martin Schröder, Jurij Henne, and Bastian Neuman, *PC-Modding* (Bonn, 2004).

104 Cf. Kai Kolwitz, 'Der PC in der Palme', *netzeitung.de*, http://www.netzeitung.de/internet/437501.html (accessed 4 September 2006).

computers in flowerpots, fire extinguishers, car tyres, beer crates, and whisky bottles.[105] Although, first and foremost, this phenomenon has to be attributed to an individual passion for arts and crafts, and to the cultivation of one's own image, this is nonetheless an activity where objects from everyday life are used differently in order to arrive at innovative solutions.

However, not only do we encounter instances of NID when it comes to sprucing up the exterior of PCs: monitors are used as notice boards covered with post-it notes, photos, or postcards. Since the screen captures the better part of our visual attention throughout the workday, the casing of monitors seems to be the perfect presentation area for everything we would like to keep an eye on. A multitude of "bits and pieces" frames our virtual workplace, reminding us of things to do at work and of those that are waiting for us afterwards, in the real world. To a certain degree this is also true for the computers themselves and for the keyboards, which, particularly if the "hunt and peck" system is used, will always briefly catch our attention. The sturdiness of monitors and computers also turns them into perfect bookends. Since they are fairly dominant on the desk anyway, any small areas and spaces below and next to them are used as storage space.

Monitors are also used for different purposes, not just for displaying information to users but also for attracting attention themselves. The luminosity of the tubes is already well known from the early period of television. Their blueish glare can be used as an excellent stroboscope light for parties by simply turning the monitor to face the wall and switching it on. Computer monitors also have the additional advantage that their luminosity can be adjusted. At one private party, for instance, two monitors featuring screen savers were used to decorate the buffet. Their red and green lighting matched the jellies on offer and invited the guests to help themselves.

In public spaces computers are also increasingly used to transmit advertising information in the form of dynamic billboards. In underground stations plasma screens supply us with the latest news and weather forecasts, or with adverts for products or local venues. In retail businesses they do not just provide us with information about opening times but also inform us of new products and how we can use them.

During the recent renovation of a small retail shop in the city centre of Cologne, a bit of imagination made up for the lack of a new shop sign: a computer screen saver announced the forthcoming shop opening. The advantages are obvious: the contents can be custom designed, time-based sequencing allows for artistic direction and information-rich communications that can be changed at any time. In this particular case the monitor could revert to its usual place and function after the completion of the renovation work.

Hardware also becomes interesting in the context of NID when it has to be scrapped. Monitor casings, for instance, are given a whole new life of their own in the form of altars from a new era that celebrate objects from an old one. Whether the

---

105   Cf. Julian Rehbinder, 'Der Computer in der Whisky-Flasche', *MSN Computer und Technik*, http://tech.de.msn. com/home/computer_article.aspx?cp-documentid=1085507 (accessed 18 October 2006).

2

3

5

1-2   Case modder Christoph Szczepinski has hidden his PC in a flowerpot, because the burgeoning PC system was becoming too much for his wife. Only around the back does the palm tree give away its secrets. A simple interior plastic bowl prevents water from soaking the computer.

3-5   Competition entries for the yearly IFA CaseCon championship, held since 2006. These home-built PCs are fully functional.

casing is illuminated, decorated with personal utensils, or simply used as a bookshelf or paper bin:[106] once gutted, there is no limit to the imagination.

At the 2005 Cebit exhibition, a recycling competition titled *Mach flott den Schrott* (Funk up that Junk) and run by the computer magazine *c't*, which is published by Heise, presented a spectrum of ideas on what can be created using old computer components. Apart from the "art" category, the "functionality" category featured a plethora of repurposing solutions with NID potential: the section about "household appliances" contained, for instance, a Pentium hotplate, a CD-solar-powered kettle, and a teapot warmer made from BNC T-components, in "sports & games" there was a scrabble game made from keys of an old keyboard, and the "house & garden" section featured a scarecrow created from CDs that were suspended from wooden branches, as well as the "P(T)ower letterbox". "We'd already put the tower including its internal components out on the street to be collected when someone placed a bundle of fly-ers on its cover. And since we [authors' note: an EDP systems company with their own workshop] actually get a lot of mail (trade journals, catalogues, and other printed mat-ter up to A3 format), we immediately came up with this idea."[107] It's a shame that the competition organisers were very keen on solutions that demonstrated a high degree of handicraft and thus simple solutions such as an old network card used as a doorstop, or the permanent magnet from a hard drive used for sticking notes to the fridge stood no chance at all and were already eliminated during the submission phase. Although none of these examples can be considered instances of spontaneous NIDs, they display the same associative ability, which is so typical for this phenomenon. Here, computer components are disassociated from their actual function and given a new lease of life through repurposing.

In Thailand, however, things are slightly more existential and exotic. There, "the market women use the battery from their mopeds to power a computer fan. A vertically set-up wire is fixed to one or two rotor blades and a chicken feather is attached to the wire's other end. The feather then circles above the goods and very effectively chases off any flies within a circle of approximately 15 centimetres. After the market has closed, the battery is put back into the moped and they drive off, thus recharging it."[108]

The huge problem of disposal[109] also forces the industry itself to come up with new concepts of recycling. Competitions are used to find new solutions based on creative

---

106 Helge: Paper bin made from monitor casing: "No joke. I use the casing of an old monitor as waste bin. The case is positioned in such a way that the screen, if it was still there, would face vertically towards the ceiling. That even looks fairly decorative.", in 'Re: Repurposing of computer parts', *Wer-weiß-was* , response to the online-ex-pert forum 'Mathematik und Physik', http://www.wer-weiss-was.de/theme50/article2648932.html (accessed 8 January 2005).

107 Ralf-Stefan Zajonc, 'Herr Würz'. Competition entry P(T)ower-Letterbox, recycling-competition 'Mach flott den Schrott' by magazine c't, Heise Zeitschriften Verlag Hanover, http://www.heise.de/ct/machflott/pro-jekte/55776 (2005).

108 Hannes Liesen, 'Re: Repurposing of computer parts', *Wer-weiß-was*, response to the online expert forum 'Mathematik und Physik', http://www.wer-weiss-was.de/theme50/article2648932.html (accessed 8 January 2005).

109 Cf. Markus Schlögl, *Recycling von Elektro- und Elektronikschrott* (Würzburg, 1995).

The P(T)ower letterbox was created from a discarded PC Tower, and now serves as the corporate letterbox for Breisach-based EDV-Systems company Zajonc + Partner.

ideas from everyday life. In addition to the traditional recycling of raw materials, there are a number of components that display useful characteristics and enough visual appeal to warrant a second lease of life after their original function has ended. Circuit boards, for instance, are turned into writing boards, and Swedish designer Torsstenson creates drinking glasses with an interesting grey-blue colour from recycled monitor panels.

However, computer hardware is generally less suitable for NID solutions compared to simple objects such as chairs, glasses, and knives. Whether this is due to its highly complex structure or its relatively short history and thus our equally young relationship with this type of object will become clearer in the future. After all, our experience in dealing with the things around us has been communicated and has matured over centuries, whereas the PC has been with us for less than one generation (the fact that a PC generation lasts less than one year and that websites have usually experienced several re-designs in spite of their short history is of no importance in this context).

NID in the Area of Computer Software – Example: Internet

The Internet is an excellent example of NID. There is hardly any other medium that displays such anarchic structures and offers so many opportunities for individual design as the global data network. Low production costs and the fact that only basic programming skills are required to distribute personal contents via the Internet have accelerated the abandonment of its original purpose. The Internet was developed in the 1950s during the cold-war period by ARPA, an agency of the American Department of Defense, with the aim of creating a network for scientists. Its decentralised structure was meant to guarantee its ability to function even in the case of a nuclear emergency. The project was successful but by now, almost 50 years later and 15 years after the development of the www, the Internet is used by all kinds of people for a multitude of purposes. In the big scheme of things, science now plays only a minor role. Today the Internet is predominantly used by private interest groups and commercial organisations. And if parts of the global network were actually sabotaged or were to fail, then we would all have a problem ...[110]

Two Internet services have also established themselves in the non-commercial sectors. We would like to introduce some NID phenomena that are related to email and the World Wide Web. However, before we do that, we take a brief look into how the Internet actually works: Internet-related programming languages are platform-independent and therefore only use ASCII text in their code. Dealing with pure text symbols has resulted, not just among users but also in the developer community, in fairly idiosyncratic approaches and applications. As with simple everyday objects, limited resources seem to boost the imagination.

---

110   Cf. René Dubach, 'Internetausfall nach 90 Min. gravierend', in *Infoweek online*, http://www.infoweek.ch/news/nw_single.cfm?news_Id=16238&sid=0 (accessed 18 July 2007).

Email

At the beginning, electronic mail was limited to pure ASCII text. There were no special characters and no font formats. One might think that, equally, there was only the written word during the era of the traditional letter. However, a person's handwriting can provide a number of clues about them. For instance, whether they were in a hurry, in a bad or good form, which age group they belong to and often it is also possible to tell which gender they are.

In order to compensate for the electronic smoothness of emails, a very particular "writing culture" has developed in this area: "smileys" or "emoticons" were invented to endow the monotonous string of characters with a certain individuality. These little line-based faces which are rotated by 90 degrees can convey digital gestures and feelings that, in online communication, substitute for the lack of facial expressions and tone of voice. Joy, sadness, irony, and anger can be communicated much better and faster than through the use of long sentences. Punctuation marks such as colon, comma, and parentheses form the basis for these typed conveyors of mood. A first collection was introduced by David Sanderson's *Smileys* featuring over 650 examples. The book has by now gained cult status and is regarded as the bible of ☺-lology. In the subtitle Sanderson even calls himself the "Noah Webster of Smileys".[111]

However, industry has managed to catch up: VoIP service provider Skype offers a broad selection of animated smileys that supply users with a large array of mood and action related icons for their chat sessions. Mobile phone manufacturers have also integrated smiley symbols into their text-messaging software including a reversing module that, on older phone models, reverts smileys back into traditional ASCII representations. And all those who are not satisfied with the same old collections of smileys can meanwhile find a multitude of ready-made smiley graphics on all sorts of topics, which can easily be copied into personal emails or chats via links on the Internet itself.[112]

Keeping things short is generally considered a standard on the Internet: abbreviations based on the sounds of letters or numbers as well as acronyms make the writing of emails more efficient and reduce the tedious pressing of keys. For example "CUL8R" stands for "see you later" and "2QT 2 B STR8" means "too cute to be straight". In this context, numbers are not used as numerals but as English language phonetic symbols (the whole phrase has to be formulated in English). Those acronyms are not always easy to decode; their meanings, however, are part of popular net culture, representing a language in their own right.

Even without acronyms, email messages often appear quite cryptic. Short, telegram-style sentences without any punctuation and featuring very idiosyncratic interpretations of orthography can sometimes be hard to unravel. Spelling has become the playground for individual preferences and evaluation criteria. Although most email programmes today ship with an integrated spellchecker that subtly underlines any

---

111   Cf. David W. Sanderson, *Smileys – Over 650, compiled by David Sanderson, the 'Noah Webster of Smileys'* (Sebastopol, 1997).

112   For further examples see for instance www.smileygarden.de, www.mysmilie.de, www.SweetIM.com, www.incredimail.com.

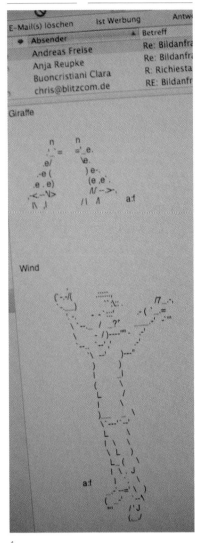

2

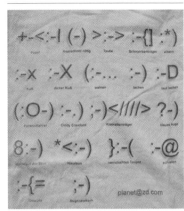

1

3

1 ASCII-art is composed of simple text characters, arranged to make up an image. With his website http://www.ascii.art.de, Andres Freise is one of the leading *gurus* of this art form.

2 The 1990s internet magazine *Planet* thanked its subscribers with a Smiley t-shirt.

3 Taking their cue from ASCII smileys, many programmes like Skype have their own smileys, used to convey people's mood.

orthographic mishaps, the suggested corrections are mostly ignored, either out of time pressure or complacency, or simply because people want to maintain their individual style of email-writing. "Emailers" who have a bit more time at their hands use the available letters and numbers for the creation of whole images and graphics, the so-called Ascii-Art.[113] Letters are integrated into these digital drawings on the basis of their shape, orientation, and optical blackness and without any regard for their phonetic values or potential word formations.

The example of email demonstrates a rather widespread, independent use of letters and language which is not considered a deliberate art form but is created, applied, and adopted anonymously, and without any professional design intervention.

Web Applications

Overall the structure and organisation of the Internet makes it fairly easy to take other people's publicly available ideas and contents and use them for one's own purposes. The structure and interpretation of HTML source code ensures that all information on the Web can be accessed. Text and images are available in digital formats and can easily be copied to one's own hard drive for further use. (However, due to numerous copyright infringements, this initial advantage has also created a number of problems and resulted in calls for a revision of the relevant legislation). The structure of hypertext enables users to access and navigate information in a non-linear way which can result in unexpected jumps and switches between different sites, pages, and offers. Thus everybody can use online information according to their own preferences, and it is even possible for users to define the way the information is displayed. On the Internet, it is the user who decides which font and font size is applied, which colour settings are used, whether images are displayed or not, and whether their own preferences can be overridden by those of the web designer.

The World Wide Web, however, is not just used for the distribution of information but also as a communication medium. In forums and chatrooms people can discuss specific subjects. However, there are often so-called "trolls" who submit any content they like and who use these forums as a platform for their narcissistic inclinations. Open access to these discussion forums makes it difficult to control and stop this kind of misappropriation. The otherwise anarchically structured Internet has, however, an ethical code named "netiquette" that calls for adherence to the unwritten rules of the online community. A very unpleasant example of netiquette infringement is "spam" (unwanted advertising) which is distributed via newsgroups, discussion forums, or email. Even secure sites cannot guarantee total freedom of such unwanted intrusion. Amongst hackers it is considered a sport to crack firewalls and place personal messages, slogans, or images on the affected sites in order to highlight security gaps. But unfortunately not all intruders are that well-meaning. There is a growing number of reports on abuses of the Web which have often become the focus of public debate. By

---

113   Cf. Polgár Tamás, *Freax the Art Album* (Winnenden, 2006) as well as further examples at: www.ascii-art.de, www.gedichte-oase.de:80/zeichenbilder.php, and www.chris.com/ascii.

now Internet crime has become rather widespread.[114] "Examples for this are filesharing, Internet fraud, computer fraud, phishing, card fraud, spying, illegal forms of pornography, identity fraud, the grooming of underage teens in chatrooms, distribution of computer viruses, of pirate copies, scams, and cyber terrorism, as well as offences such as incitement or libel."[115]

As welcome as the cheap alternative to traditional telephony may be, it, too, is being overshadowed by the first cases of abuse: fraudsters have discovered this new form of telecommunication for their own ends. They eavesdrop on conversations that contain confidential information, or send emails asking the recipient to submit account details via a fake bank phone number. They use caller ID spoofing to hide their true identity by using arbitrarily selected phone numbers as their own and alter their voice which, through the use of software, can even be changed from male to female, or vice versa. Less damaging but nonetheless unpleasant is "spit" (Spam over Internet Telephony), which has not yet reached Germany but has, so far, interrupted the sleep of many a US VoIPer (Voice over Internet Protocol; here used as a noun for those who use Internet telephony) in order to tell them, via recorded messages, about alleged lottery wins, illegal software, or products for penis enlargement.[116]

In the context of gender, the Internet also offers some new possibilities:[117] So-called "avatars" enable users to adopt another personality for communicating in virtual spaces. Net users can become heroes of their own, but also of the opposite, gender. Even in regular chat groups, users can never be certain whether their fellow chatters, who often use a fake name, are at least of the gender they pretend to be. Particularly during the early, male-dominated period of the Net, many men tried to benefit from their anonymity by attracting more attention through posing as females. In those cases name, gender, age, and so forth were altered with the aim of getting more rapid answers to personal questions, or attracting more conversation partners in online discussions but also in order to fulfil a secret desire for being somebody else or, on the one hand, to avoid sexual harassment (usually the reason why women pretend to be men) and, on the other hand, to experience an erotic stimulus (often the reason why men pretend to be women). Whatever the reasons, assuming a (fake) gender role seems to be a rather joyful and harmless experience.

---

114   Cf. Alfred Krüger, *Angriffe aus dem Netz (TELEPOLIS) – Die neue Szene des digitalen Verbrechens* (Hanover, 2006); Thor Alexander, *Das große Sicherheitsbuch – So schützen Sie Ihren Computer und Ihre Privatsphäre im Internet* (Berlin, 2005); Tarik Ahmia, 'Tatort Cyberspace, Internet-Kriminalität und Online-Terrorismus', *Das Parlament no. 34–35*, http://www.das-parlament.de/2006/34-35/thema/029.html (accessed 21 August 2006); Bundesministerium des Innern, 'Internetkriminalität', http://www.bmi.bund.de/cln_012/nn_122688/sid_2DACFE953F755198BF9E00FBCC5E51E6/Internet/Content/Themen/Kriminalitaet/DatenundFakten/Internetkriminalitaet__Id__94087__de.html (accessed 6 June 2004).

115   'Internetkriminalität', in *Wikipedia, Die freie Enzyklopädie*, http://de.wikipedia.org/wiki/Internetkriminalit%C3%A4t (accessed 1 October 2007).

116   Cf. Ulrich Hottelet, 'Cyber-Räuber am Draht', *Die Zeit*, no. 29, http://www.zeit.de/2006/29/Voice-over-IP 2006.

117   Cf. Sherry Turkle, *Leben im Netz. Identität in Zeiten des Internet* (Reinbek by Hamburg, 1998).

Website Production

Design and production always have to catch up with the development of new technologies. This was also true for the early period of the World Wide Web. There was no software that would allow for intuitive web design.[118] "QuarkXPress" was used for layout purposes with the important add-ons of being able to define a page format that spread over double the height of a monitor and of specifying the traditional print-related size format of millimetres in points. "Photoshop" is still an essential tool for layout and image processing purposes. Besides being able to create screen layouts, it offers palettes of web-safe colours and can convert images into web standards such as jpeg or gif. (Today, Photoshop offers numerous additional features for web publishing.) An ingenious side effect of these new image and text formats, such as Adobe's "PDF" for instance, is that exploding file sizes have been shrunk to a fraction of their original size.

Since HTML itself consists of pure text symbols each simple text processing tool that could produce ASCII code, such as "SimpleText" for example, could be used for web programming. Although a plethora of web editors and web-ready image processing tools are available today, it is still possible to use pre-web software for text-based programming languages such as HTML, DHTML, or Javascript. However, it is doubtful that anyone would still do this since the number of web programming languages is consistently rising and thus it would be too difficult to be up to speed on the entire repertoire. Testing a website at home is also easily achieved since it can be called up from the hard drive and displayed in a browser.

A creative repurposing of code became necessary not only within programmes but also in the context of general programming. Since HTML was developed by technologists and not by designers there was hardly any design thinking involved in the creation of programming languages. Before the advent of Javascript and Cascading Style Sheets the possibilities were very limited, which was certainly also related to a lack of design vocabulary amongst IT specialists. The few options for displaying type resulted in a practice where important font styles such as headers, navigation labels and wordmarks were integrated as images. Tables were also used in similar ways. Originally developed to display complex tabular relationships such as the periodic system for instance, web designers soon discovered that the tables' grey frames could be switched off thus providing new layout options. Elements such as images and text blocks could be placed next to one another, text could be set in columns, and screen layouts could be defined by pixels. Since whitespace, meaning empty table cells, was not supported by all browsers, transparent images or letters of the same colour as the background were used as placeholders. Frames, which are used for defining the placement of contents from several sites within one browser window, allowed for the combination of contents from different sources. But they were also used for purely decorative purposes as was exemplified by one of the first versions of the website by furniture manufacturer Vitra: through the use of frames, they developed their individual colour matrix.

---

118   Cf. David Siegel, *Web Site Design. Killer Web Sites* (Munich, 1998).

All these examples demonstrate that, during the early period of the Web, there was a multitude of instances where programmes and programming code was repurposed. Without this talent for improvisation, it would not have been possible to implement many of the early website designs or at least they would have looked quite different. Thus the Internet is a good example for the success of anonymous changes of use because many of the solutions described above were developed by someone and simultaneously discovered by many others, then copied until they eventually became established forms of repurposing, similar to the redesign of objects. Although the Internet is a fairly recent medium, its history of use reveals established patterns of behaviour which suggests that NID as a human ability is not only applied in the context of products but also in the use of language and virtual spaces.

The Subjects: Objects of, and Reasons for, Repurposing

Without any doubt, repurposing objects is closely related to cultural, climatic, financial, and also personal conditions. Since this study primarily deals with everyday instances of repurposing in affluent, technological societies, we would once more like to point out that the people whose repurposing behaviour is discussed here neither live in so-called "third world" countries, nor do they suffer from any other kind of deprivation. We are therefore dealing with the question why people, despite being able to buy specific objects for each of their needs, still frequently, be it consciously or subconsciously, repurpose existing things.

Methodology

We designed a questionnaire in order to find out which objects are repurposed at home. The questionnaire was sent out via email to about 250 people, most of them students at the Köln International School of Design (KISD), who, due to the nature of their course, are familiar with questions of design and therefore, we hoped, were in a position not only to tell us about their repurposing behaviour, but also about what motivated them to do so. Our sample, therefore, has a particular interest in design and cannot be considered representative in demographic terms. We deliberately chose a group of people who can be assumed to have a higher degree of awareness regarding their relationship to the designed environment.

The questionnaire was constructed in such a way that repurposed objects should be listed according to specific areas in the home. During the test phase, we realised that it was difficult for many people to identify their own NID behaviour and therefore we provided some helpful suggestions: We listed typical objects and functions according to the areas or rooms to which they usually belong, and we also provided additional space for the respondents to list their own so-called "personal NIDs".

Since we were not only interested in instances of NID as such, but also in the underlying motivations, we provided a list of potential reasons (lack of space, convenience, economics, personal persuasion, creativity, ecology, individuality, mobility) next to each field and asked people to select the most appropriate one. Finally, we asked respondents for their "favourite NID" and for any additional remarks.

Gender comparison was very important for us. The questionnaire was sent to 125 women and 125 men; of those, 16 women and 14 men responded, giving a response rate of 12% (12.8% for women and 11.2% for men). In relation to the total number of people contacted, this result cannot be considered representative. However, 30 completed questionnaires are enough to let us draw relevant conclusions in the context of our subject area.

The Sample

Before analysing the results in terms of gender, we would like to talk about some limitations, problems, and ambivalences.

As mentioned earlier, our sample has two specific characteristics. It consists of young women and men (approximately in their early twenties to early thirties) who are either studying at university level or have recently graduated. Therefore, we are dealing with well-educated people who, due to their age, are future-oriented but, for the most part, do not yet have a lot of money at their disposal. Consequently, we can assume that their lifestyle is both modern and improvised. The openness of an as yet not established way of interacting with things signifies both a constraint and an intention. It is, however, impossible to decide for each individual case which of these two factors is the predominant one, and to what degree. Potential constraints arise from financial restrictions, and the intention often originates from the social impetus to reject prevalent consumerist conventions.

The professional perspective reinforces the unconventional aspect and also that of a more direct and conscious interaction with the world of objects: Designers and design students usually possess a more differentiated view, as well as a more refined perception, of the world of objects, because not only do they use things, they also create them. And they do so, primarily, as professionals and not as hobbyists.

Selecting a sample like this one obviously has its advantages and disadvantages. However, we believe that the advantages clearly outweigh the disadvantages. It is de facto correct that our survey is limited to a particular group, but the conclusion that the results can therefore not be generalised and are not suitable for revealing particular trends lacks substance. This deliberately chosen limitation at the same time raises the expected quality of the responses, because the refined awareness and competence regarding the world of objects mentioned earlier is necessary to fully understand the rather unusual questions we asked. Besides, this is an explorative study which, for the first time, tries to approach this subject area and does so by using empirical methods.

Lastly, one could argue that questioning young designers, who deal with the design of things in a conceptional and reflected way on an everyday basis, might elicit responses that are possibly too sophisticated and not "spontaneous" enough to capture the essence of Non-Intentional Design.

The evaluation of the questionnaires, however, showed that, on the one hand, being professionals was helpful in understanding our questions, and, on the other hand, did not get in the way of practising NID.

As far as gender was concerned, our questions were deliberately formulated in a neutral manner. Earlier experiences in the context of gender-specific inquiries had brought up a peculiar ambivalence towards the category of gender: The more explicit the question of gender was addressed, the stronger the resistance became to grant this aspect any real influence in our everyday lives. The fact that negating the importance of gender is theoretically and empirically untenable has been proven by numerous statistics, surveys, and gender studies, and therefore does not need to be elaborated on any further in this context. It seems more useful to try and analyse the motives which lead to a rationalisation or, at best, marginalisation, of the topos of gender when the issue is addressed directly. Our studies revealed a common form of defence that hypostatised the individual, in particular within the framework of professional life and the job market, which could be summarised thus: Rather than on gender, job opportunities, competencies, and forms of cooperation depended far more on individual disposition; there were no preferences or disadvantages in relation to gender, what was important were the behaviour and the actions of the individual.

The reasons for these "general human qualities" statements must, however, be differentiated when it comes to gender and age: Since men do not usually experience any gender-related disadvantages, the scope of their imagination regarding this topic is somewhat limited. A different rejection pattern can be observed with young women. They are in the process of breaking away from gender-specific types of education and jobs, and want to be successful and establish themselves independently of their sex. Therefore, they react to questions which might refer to any potential gender-specific discrimination with a great deal of suspicion, or dismiss them as obsolete and more relevant to the generation of their mothers. We assume (and understand) that they do not want to be disencouraged from forging ahead and making a successful living as women. They are, or at least think they are, confident enough to master their private and professional lives independently of their sex and therefore do not want to be confronted constantly with these issues.

This is especially true for our sample: female designers or design students who have chosen a modern profession and a contemporary design education that has overcome traditional gender-specific specialisations (e.g. so-called domestic domains, or those related to decoration and accessories, such as textile, fashion, or jewellery design, in comparison to "male", technology-oriented segments, such as industrial or automobile design). On the other hand, these women are nonetheless confronted every day with gender-specific situations or discrimination in their personal and professional lives, and are able to specify differences, hierarchies, or evaluations related to gender when this issue is either addressed indirectly, or in the context of other questions and experiences.

With our questions on the subject of NID we could circumvent this potential ambivalence without creating any methodological complications, because there was no need to make the gender discussion a subject in its own right. Of course we asked for people's sex when collecting the usual demographic data, but otherwise this subject was not specifically addressed in our questions. Sampling the sex of our subjects was sufficient to analyse potential differences in the frequency, locality, contents, and kinds of NID practice.

Spaces and Rooms

Most instances of NID could be identified in the kitchen. Out of 30 responses, an average of 54.3% of descriptions were related to the kitchen: 60% of the respondents use NIDs instead of oven mitts, another 60% for the storage of provisions, 57% as substitute for flower vases, a further 53% listed alternatives for ashtrays and candleholders, and 43% for wastebins.

The home office came second in terms of frequency of changes of use: 60% of the sample used alternative items for opening letters, 60% used NIDs for the storage of pens or notes, 37% substituted bookends and 10% used alternatives for shelves. This amounts to an average of 46.8% of NIDs in the home office.

Next up is the bedroom with a similar average percentage (46.6%) of instances of repurposing: 60% of respondents reported the use of NIDs for bedside tables, 57% for storing clothes, and 23% used alternative beds.

It can be assumed that both kitchen and bedroom are places with a high NID potential because they represent particularly private areas within the home. Homeowners might feel that, in these rooms, they have more freedom to interact with objects than in those areas that are also used by guests, such as the hall. The latter has the lowest NID rating with an average of only 18.5%. In our sample the home office represents the most used room, since the majority of respondents are design students who do not have a separate office and work from home instead. This might also explain the high number of NID instances in this area.

Gender Comparison of Instances of Repurposing by Room or Space

First of all, we saw that women answered the questionnaires in a more detailed manner than men. Altogether they listed more instances of NID and also more reasons for their implementation. A comparison of the rooms for which NIDs were listed, results in the following proportions: In the kitchen (women: 58.6%; men: 50%), the living room (women: 37.8%; men: 28.8%), and in the bedroom (women: 50.6%; men: 42.6%) the percentage of NIDs is roughly balanced between the sexes, if we take into account that men responded with a lesser degree of detail. Although there were altogether only two more female respondents than male ones, the women listed 82 more instances of NID than the men. (From a total of 478 NIDs, 280 were specified by women and "only" 198 by men.)

In the home office (women: 46.4%; men: 47%) and in the hall (women:19%; men:18%) the percentages are similar. As far as these spaces are concerned, the detailed responses by women suggest that men are responsible for comparably more instances of NID in these areas than women. If we look at the order in which rooms are named as places of NID, then, for men, the home office comes second after the kitchen, whereas it only takes fifth place, after the bathroom, for women. Here, two different interpretations are possible which are hard to differentiate: it might be that the work space – in keeping with traditional gender roles – is indeed more important for men than for women, although all respondents are either students or professionals.

"I've noticed that in 90% of bathrooms,
the cleaning cloth is always hung over the wash-
basin's U-bend – does that count?"

[Respondent 13, male, from NID-questionnaire]

It might also be that the difference is related less to the intensity of work than to the importance attributed to it. If the latter is true, then we can say that men still identify themselves more strongly with this domain and feel more at home there than women. Another possible explanation is that women separate workspace more clearly from private space and therefore design this area in a more professional way, thereby keeping it relatively free from instances of repurposing in the sense of NID.

It is also interesting to break up the results according to the objects involved: For the home office, women specified more changes of use for storing pens, opening letters, and writing notes, whereas men quoted more NIDs for shelving. Storing pens, opening letters, and making notes are activities that need little room. Shelves, however, are more bulky. Therefore we might suggest that the workplaces of men take up more space than those of women. This is confirmed by our additional observations in different homes. There are two areas that show clearly different percentages in instances of repurposing: women listed significantly more NIDs in the bathroom (women: 48.5%; men: 34%), on the balcony, and in the garden (women: 56.3%; men: 26%). The high number of NIDs in the bathroom implemented by women might be a result of the larger range of products for women in this area. It can also be assumed that women spend more time in this space than men. The fact that women know more NID tricks for warding off pests, and altogether specified a higher number of NIDs for balconies and gardens, indicates that they keep more plants in their living area and are more familiar with taking care of them.

As far as the other rooms are concerned, it is worthwhile differentiating between individual objects. Female respondents listed more NIDs for oven mitts, for storing provisions, for ashtrays, vases, and wastebins in the kitchen whereas the result for candleholders is more balanced.

In the bedroom, women specified more NIDs for their wardrobes, beds, and bedside tables than men. However, taking into account that there were more female respondents, the ratio of repurposing other objects to function as beds is comparable with 4 out of 16 women and 3 out of 14 men listing their respective NIDs.

In the living room, the percentage of NIDs related to the storage of items is identical. For shelves and lamps men specified more NIDs, whereas women came first with alternatives for curtains and seating. Here, we can assume that the latter are more often used and designed by women since these objects mainly fulfil decorative purposes. Lamps and shelves, however, are more closely related to the technical sphere. This points towards women using NIDs in the living room in order to create more atmosphere and convenience, while the NIDs described by men refer to the male passion for handicraft and DIY. Heubach analyses the hobbyist phenomenon of "eternal" tinkering in stating that "it represents the attempt to transform the act of setting-oneself-to-work into an independent and eternal condition."[119]

---

119   Friedrich Heubach, *Das bedingte Leben. Theorie der psycho-logischen Gegenständlichkeit der Dinge* (Munich, 1987), p. 144.

"With me, it always has to be about speed. (For instance, I'll use a T-shirt instead of an oven glove, because I don't want to look for oven gloves that always seem to be in the wash."

[Respondent 02, female, from NID-questionnaire]

Repurposed Objects

When reviewing all quoted NIDs, some clear favourites emerge: Regardless of space and gender, chairs are very often used for purposes other than sitting; many respondents specified NIDs for the storage of objects of all kinds, and paper knives are hardly used at all, instead they are replaced by fingers, pens, or other longish objects.

Gender Comparison of Instances of Repurposing

From a total of 28 suggested changes of use, 19 were implemented predominantly by women, 2 equally by both sexes, and only 6 were implemented more often by men. Among these 6, one object, the shelving, appears twice.

Objects which are more often replaced by men include: bookends, lamps, shelves in the living room and home office, and wardrobes. The difference is most pronounced in the case of shelves. If we look at the items that are quoted as alternatives, then men mainly listed zinc cellar shelves and (cardboard) boxes. Women quoted more unusual replacements such as cable reels, stones and wooden boards, and a "self-built" shelf that came without any further explanation.

Four men and 4 women listed alternatives for industrially produced lamps. In terms of percentages, men are in first place again. One of them, however, seems to have misunderstood the question because he quoted "IKEA". The other alternatives listed are: "roof gutter", "light bulb", and "desk lamp on guitar amplifier". Of the 4 women, two listed "light bulb", one quoted "spotlight", and the fourth had welded her lamp herself. Here, male NIDs are more unusual while the women resorted to rather simple solutions.

The same picture emerges when looking at alternatives for wardrobes. Four representatives of each sex use makeshift wardrobes. For men these are: a wine shelf, a shelf, coat hangers hooked to a ring binder, and a steel rope; the women quoted a gas boiler, a towel rail, nails, and an ironing board. Although the overall number of responses is too low to be able to draw general conclusions, we can nonetheless state that the men's solutions are again more complex than the women's, or maybe just more complicated, since steel ropes and wine shelves both need fitting before they can be used. The women's NIDs are comparably simpler. Ironing boards and gas boilers are likely to be located in the hall anyway and can thus be temporarily repurposed as wardrobes. It is not difficult to hammer a few nails into a wall, and a towel rail can easily be fitted. The wardrobe, therefore, seems to be the only object on whose design men seem to spend more time than women.

"Equipment is not just a question of money, it's also about taste and lifestyle. Bookends are conservative, those beakers for toothbrushes are just so middle class!"

[Respondent 06, male, from NID-questionnaire]

"Mostly, you just do it without thinking about it, when you use something, such as the shower-curtain rail to dry towels, or a newspaper as a fly swatter, and so on."

[Respondent 07, female, from NID-questionnaire]

Personal NIDs and Favourite NIDs

If we take a closer look at the changes of use in the two categories "Personal NIDs" and "Favourite NIDs", then it looks as though women are more concerned about aesthetically pleasing solutions when designing their homes. While men quoted boxes or cardboard boxes as alternatives for storage relatively frequently, we hardly find any boxes in female homes. Men also quoted NIDs like "balcony as garbage dump" or "bathroom as storage room". Fairy lights used instead of light bulbs, and a "decorative shawl" as an alternative sunscreen are NIDs implemented by women. Women also quoted significantly more instances of repurposing that are related to body and hair care, for example: "body oil as bath oil", "Nivea cream as hair gel", "pen as hair pin", "hair tie made from socks", "flower pot as storage for mascara and hairbrush", "jewellery in coffee cup", and "mirror as hanger for necklaces".

The most popular changes of use for both sexes were "chair as ladder", "bottle as hammer", and "paper clips or pegs to close bags".

Reasons for Repurposing

The question of what lies behind changes of use touches upon the areas of design, psychology, and sociology. In a design-oriented context it seems feasible to focus first on visible phenomena and leave the interpretation of use aside for now.

We have already excluded deliberate changes of use. They are not part of NID, our research area, which is concerned with everyday, non-intentional changes of use. In these instances of repurposing, which are carried out sub-consciously in the sense that the people who implement them consider their actions "normal" and everyday, related motivations tend to be obscured, hence people are not aware of them. Additionally, there are many forms of repurposing that have become so established that they are perceived as "correct" use, for example, stacking objects on a chair.

Preferences

Non-intentional design oscillates between conscious and sub-conscious actions, and we can rarely tell by simply looking at repurposed objects why they were used in that way. And most people who implement changes of use are often not able to analyse why they did so in retrospect.

The evaluation of our questionnaires confirms this issue. It was obvious that many of the respondents were not able to clearly identify their motivations. This is borne out by the fact that some people left the motivation column blank. The majority (29%) of those who quoted reasons listed "lack of space"; almost as many (23%) settled on "convenience", followed by "economy" (17%), "personal persuasion" (9%), "creativity" (6.7%), "individuality" (6%), "ecology" (5.6%), and "mobility" in last place with 4%.

The frequency of "lack of space" as a reason for repurposing objects can be explained by the characteristics of our sample – it consists of young people, most of whom live in just one room for financial reasons and therefore do not have much space. The same issues are likely to be behind the third most frequent motivation, "economy". Hence therefore, the second-most quoted motivation, "convenience" (23%), has to be attributed particular significance. If we work on the assumption that our sample group will have sufficient space and money in the foreseeable future, and consequently both of the motivations "lack of space" and "economy" will become less relevant, then we are left with "convenience". This corresponds to what we have learned from many informal interviews, where the most frequently mentioned reason for repurposing things was described as not having the "correct" object at hand when needed. We can therefore assume that convenience generally tends to be one of the main motivations for NIDs in developed societies.

Although we were not quite happy with using the term "convenience" in our questionnaires because of potential negative connotations such as listlessness and lethargy, or even laziness, this reason was cited very often. On the one hand, this might imply that many people do not mind being considered lazy, on the other hand, they might have referred to the true meaning of the word in the sense of effortlessness and simplicity, or in short, selected the term as referring to the option that afforded the least effort.

Gender Comparison of Reasons for Repurposing

The hierarchy of motivations is similar for women and men. For men, "lack of space" is in first place, followed by "convenience", "economy", "personal persuasion", "individuality", "creativity", "ecology", and "mobility". For women, the order of the first two items is reversed, "convenience" comes before "lack of space", with "economy" in third place, again followed by "creativity", "personal persuasion", "ecology", "individuality", and "mobility" once more last. There are no significant differences but ecological and creative aspects might play a slightly more important role for women. Although men mentioned "individuality" less often in terms of percentages, it takes fifth place in the male hierarchy, whereas it ranks seventh for women. Therefore we can say that for men "personal persuasion" and "individuality" are more important motivations for repurposing things. Both of these terms point to a less spontaneous interaction with objects than is indicated in the aspect of "convenience", which appears to be slightly more relevant for women. We can thus assume that, on average, men spend more time implementing changes in the world of objects than women, and that the latter tend to interact with things in a more spontaneous manner.

When taking into account all the above-mentioned and analysed aspects in order to arrive at a conclusion about gender differences, then we can clearly state that, overall, as well as in certain details, women implement more changes of use in their homes than men. They obviously seem to be more concerned with, and spend more time on the design of their homes. This is an aspect professional design and industry should take note of and regard women as an important target group for interior-design products.

Exemplary Target Group Differentiation: Nationality, Profession, Age

Users can be assigned to certain categories. Depending on people's social and cultural background there are specific, traditional NIDs, a few examples of which will be introduced in the following passage.

Example: Nationality

Using and repurposing things changes according to the meaning and value that is attributed to objects in different cultures. This is not only true for cultures that differ greatly. Relevant examples can be found nearby: In Germany, for instance, cars are cult objects with an almost holy aura, whereas in the Romance countries they are considered objects of daily use. This can be observed when looking at the differences in parking behaviour in Germany and Italy. Whereas in Germany people go to extra lengths in order not to touch the car in front of or behind them, it is common practice in Italy to unlock the hand brake and set the gear to neutral in order to allow for others to push the car forwards or backwards without effort when needed. In Germany cars have a much more private character than in Italy. There, people communicate with other traffic participants by sounding their horn or, in the case of bad driving or similar, shouting through open windows. In Germany people tend to drive with their windows closed (probably also due to the colder climate) and tend to interact with the objects inside the car such as the stereo or the navigation system.

The different appreciation of cars also results in different types of repurposing. Unlike in Germany, a small scratch or dent is no issue at all in Italy, and therefore you will generally see more people there leaning against their own or other people's cars. It is also more common in Italy than in Germany to transport bulky items in a passenger car (with open roof or boot).

Example: Profession

Some instances of repurposing have established themselves in certain professions but are not implemented outside the work environment. In pubs or restaurants, for instance, it is common practice to clean ashtrays with paintbrushes. However, no waiter or waitress would do the same at home because the repurposing of paintbrushes as a cleaning utensil serves to save time in environments where a large number of ashtrays have to be cleaned several times a day. At home this is usually not necessary. Other professions have their own "inherited" changes of use, which can only be observed within the respective professional environments. Musicians, for instance, use many forms of repurposing: violinists often put a handkerchief between their chin and the instrument in order to protect the former; drummers use sweaters and pieces of fabric to mute their instruments; guitarists use coins when there is no plectrum to hand. Further common changes of use can be observed in the skilled trades. Tailors, for instance, use soap for drawing patterns – often on newspapers; chefs pit cherries with hairpins and fix roulades with toothpicks, which are also used on olives in Martinis. Carpenters use their yardsticks to open beer bottles and a knife to sharpen their pencils. Architects build their models from old cardboard boxes, and for an even distribution of chalk on their blueprints they might reach for a piece of cotton wool. Gardeners and farmers tie up branches with nylons, drown snails in beer-filled yoghurt pots and build scarecrows using old clothing, straw, and aluminium foil.

Example: Age Group

Age is also an important factor regarding different types of repurposing. For small children, shape is the primary criterion when using objects. A table makes an excellent house, because it has a roof as soon as you crawl under it. A laundry basket can be a boat, because it has a similar shape. So tins and pots become drums, wooden spoons are turned into drumsticks, yoghurt pots become telephones, and beds are used as trampolines. Older children often build toys from materials that were discarded by their parents, or from things they find. This serves to counteract a lack or to test one's own skilfulness in comparison to other kids.

From a certain age onwards, roughly around the time we start school, our relationship with things changes dramatically. Frequently prestige now plays a central role. Changes of use now serve to express membership of a certain group, an attitude, or an opinion. Teen fashions often comprise the repurposing of certain things, such as cutting off a normal pair of jeans and wearing them as shorts, wearing safety pins as earrings, colouring hair with food colours, or putting it up with a pencil, de-colouring fabrics with bleach, braiding bracelets from darning cotton, using all sorts of small boxes instead of buying pencil cases, and writing slogans or messages on trousers, backpacks, and shoes. Lack of money will certainly play a role in all this as well since most teenagers are still dependent on pocket money from their parents.

When leaving school, changes of use based on profession, gender, and culture become more prevalent than those based on age. Older, retired people, however, will again tend to use things in non-intended ways, often because there is a lack of adequately designed objects for this age group, or because they are used to keeping and reusing things due to shortages they experienced in the postwar period. But maybe they have simply developed a more relaxed attitude towards things, and are therefore able to interact more freely with them by using the shopping trolley as a crutch, the magnifying glass as spectacles, or the TV as a conversation partner.

2

4

7

6

1 Wastebins marking out the goal
2 Collapsible box as playboat
3 Blanket as Red Riding Hood costume

4 Newspaper protecting against spray
5 Dog collar as necklaces
6 Odds and ends as rucksack decoration and personal statement
7 Identity band as key- and lighter chain

The Letter Opener

" ...

There are some things that we own, but forget about because we do not use them. The purpose for which they were invented, or the work which they are supposed to do or facilitate can be done without them, no matter how badly, clumsily, or grudgingly. [...] Take, for example, the activity of opening letters. Almost everybody owns a letter opener but hardly anyone uses it. [...] So we make do with whatever is at hand, some other kind of knife, scissors, the handle of a spoon, or a knitting needle – even a pencil or pen, or we use our index finger by squeezing it into a corner of the envelope and ripping it open. Rrrrip! Letter openers really come into their own when you cannot think of a gift idea. And surprisingly enough, they are also some of the most appealing: available in a multitude of shapes, colours, designs, and materials.
Designers are tirelessly reinventing the very same object. Recently I watched someone take a letter opener and look at it contemplatively. Suddenly he clasped it with his fist, raised his arm towards his wife and smiled at her: 'Now, if I were to ....'.
A letter opener is a tame knife. Or a knife in disguise.

"
...

Manfred Sack, *Alltagssachen. Eine Sammlung von allerlei notwendigen Gebrauchsgegenständen* (Vienna 1992) p. 68/69.

The Objects

After having studied NID users, we will now turn our attention to objects and their suitability for Non-Intentional Design. We want to find out which types of objects are used most, and which less often in the context of NID. In order to do so we have divided objects into product groups that display certain similarities regarding their suitability for NID.

When analysing objects, it is important to remember that it is not sufficient just to look at their form and function. We always have to consider these two attributes in the context of actual user interaction. "It has become clear, however, that the objects themselves are not essential, that the objects in and of themselves are nothing as long as they are not viewed in the context of their relationship with the users."[120]

The recognition and evaluation of objects, as well as the creation of new things, are not always rooted in deliberation and personal creative efforts. More often than not we imitate things we have seen before or apply things we have learned. This is not only true of the use of products but also of changes of use.

"There is definitely no freedom when using objects. [...] The relationship is rather similar to an old marriage where there is no hope for a liberating divorce: We could not live without the help and the resistance of objects, and without us the existence of objects would be meaningless. [...] They define use through their cultural predetermination, they are provoked and assimilated by individual and collective needs."[121]

Objects change together with mankind. Newly discovered materials, techniques, and skills can improve existing products, or call for new ones. Human needs always have an effect on the world of products. Therefore, an analysis that focuses solely on objects will not suffice in capturing their meaning. Museums of cultural history, for instance, confront us with this false conclusion when we walk through rooms filled with glass cabinets. Without any explanatory texts and images that demonstrate the application and value of the exhibited objects, those objects remain a mystery to us. Due to a lack of knowledge about their application, the objects, at first glance, appear useless to us. "The original proximity or distance between humans and their objects can hardly be perceived in a museum. Neither does it communicate how the relationship between people and things has changed over the centuries, nor which scrutinizing glances and gestures were used to evaluate things. [...]Placing an object in a museum means taking it out of its original context and into a new one which significantly changes its reality."[122]

It is easier for us to imagine an object's use if, in our cultural environment, similar forms are still used for the same function. Based on our own product experience, we are able to recognise knives and weapons from the Stone Age, cooking utensils, antique jugs, jewellery, or coins. (In the case of old tools for a meanwhile obsolete or

120   Bazon Brock, 'Zur Archäologie des Alltags', in *Das gewöhnliche Design., Friedrich Friedl and Gerd Ohlhauser, Documentation of an exhibition of the School of Design at Fachhochschule Darmstadt 1976*, (Cologne, 1979), p. 24.

121   Gert Selle, *Siebensachen. Ein Buch über die Dinge* (Frankfurt, 1997), p. 19 f.

122   Ibid., p. 53. Here, Selle quotes Eva Sturm (1990).

forgotten craft, however, it will be harder, if not impossible, for us to identify their practical value.)

We seem to have developed a close relationship with these objects; their use has prevailed throughout the centuries. Only their shape and handling have changed in accordance with our own evolution "in the same way that the gesture of drinking is related to an endless variety of forms for the respective appliances, which all go back to some ancient shape of a clay receptacle and eventually to the concave shape of a cupped hand."[123]

The associative ability that enables us to attribute particular uses to objects from bygone eras, and the abstraction necessary to be able to identify a practical value from small pieces and shards, are both preconditions for the phenomenon of NID. Because, in the same way in which the objects have been subject to evolution, we could always fall back on their earlier forms in order to fulfil a related need.

Simple Things

The product category of simple things that derives from these considerations is usually juxtaposed with basic needs essential for survival. These include bowls, mugs, and glasses for drinking, knives for cutting foodstuffs or as tools to separate materials, areas suitable for sitting or lying in order to rest, surfaces for placing or storing things, as well as containers for arranging and storing our possessions. Ever since humans have owned things we have been familiar with them, and have learned and experienced their use either in predefined or ad hoc ways.

Changes of use in the sense of NID happen in such a natural way that more often than not we do not even notice them. A chair whose backrest is used for drying towels, or on which we stand while changing a light bulb, or which we use as a rack for jackets or bags seems hardly worthy of being the object of a research project – this, at least, was a reaction we encountered when explaining the term NID to others.

Only when we mentioned more exotic instances of repurposing, such as using the glass from washing machine doors as salad bowls or casseroles, did people become more interested. As a result, when asked to spontaneously name some personal NIDs, people tended to list individual changes of use that entailed some personal creative effort rather than collective instances of NID.

It seems therefore fair to assume that we, regarding our use of basic forms, not only consider their original applications as self-evident functions but also the related options of repurposing. Although these objects were only created for a specific basic need, they have, over time, developed into multi-functional ones that have more than just one potential use. For us a chair is no longer just a chair but also a stepladder, a clothes rack, a gymnastics bar, or a shelf. These multiple uses work best when using an archetypical chair with a solid seat, backrest, and four legs. Rollers, armrests,

123   Ibid., p. 76.

4

Alternative Places for Books

1 Radiator as bookshelf
2 Sofa as bookshelf
3 Wine crate as bookshelf
4 Chair as bookshelf

decorative elements, or ergonomic versions, as well as high-tech accessories tend to significantly reduce the number of possible functions.

Cheap Products and Disposable Products

Another product group is worth a closer look in the framework of NID: cheap products that are flooding the market and are mainly sold in chain stores. A low price is often an incentive to buy. Many bargains find their way into our trolley on the pretext that we will either change any objectionable detail, or amend any minor faults until they fully meet our expectations. If these experiments fail, or if we do not need the product any more, we can simply throw it away because it "did not cost us" anything. Low investment results in our being more ruthless with things: We often use cheap products for rinsing paint brushes, as beakers for toothbrushes, cleaning buckets, cleaning rags, and so forth, because using grandma's collector's cups to rinse paintbrushes seems downright stupid. "For instance, the reason that throwaway furniture remained in fashion with particular social groups over a period of eight years is that this furniture, in terms of its material qualities, was clearly predestined for destruction, or for an appropriation that could go as far as destruction. It facilitates the enforcement of one's intention to appropriate because it is cheap. Hence it can easily be replaced."[124] While the repurposing of cheap products fills us with pride when we have managed to appropriate them and endow these worthless objects with meaning, we consider existing assets worthy of being preserved because we experience their loss as painful. With cheap products, it is we who dominate them, whereas expensive objects demand that we treat them with respect. In the latter case, therefore, freedom of use, and thus also the potential for NID applications, is largely compromised.

A similar potential for changes of use can also be found with old, second-hand products that are available at low cost. What some consider rubbish might still be of use to others for whom the repurposing of old things is a passion and part of their way of life. For these people attics, cellars, and in particular flea markets are true treasure troves. It is exactly the patina and run-down, historically charged charm of these second-hand objects that makes them so attractive. More often than not, people already envision during the act of purchasing what they can do with those relics from bygone times because they are rarely used according to their original purpose. Old milk churns are turned into umbrella stands or vases for dried flowers, cartwheels become lamp shades, old chests of drawers are transformed into hi-fi shelves, grandma's blouse is resurrected as a fashionable summer top, and an old army backpack gets a new lease of life as a satchel. After some adding to and taking away, some replacing parts and repairing, the new owners can proudly present what they have managed to create from an object destined for the wastebin. Bulk waste that was put out on the street for collection represents an even more demanding resource to challenge people's fantasy and

---

124   Bazon Brock, '*Zur Archäologie des Alltags*' (loc.cit.), p. 30 f.

2

Makeshift Solutions – Emergency Help

The following uses are all examples of temporary NIDs. In response to a certain situation, solutions were found that will fulfil their purpose only for a short time. Paper cups and empty bottles or drink cans get used as ashtrays, towels as salad spinners or oven gloves, a rubber mallet crushes ice, and flowers get watered with teapots and cafetières.

Even disposable packaging gets used in many ways, as various examples demonstrate: a wine bottle as a candle holder or flower vase, an empty pickle jar as a paint pot, or for storing buttons, loose change, pens and pencils, screws and various odds and ends.

4

1 Water bottles as flower vases
2 Coke bottle as flower vase
3 Paper cup as ashtray
4 Wine bottle as candle holder
5 Disposable jars for screw and bolt storage
6 Yoghurt pot as paint pot

6

The Bottle

"
. . .

Those empty bottles which are kept with the aim of using them for purposes not intended by their producers, e.g. as candleholders, flowerpots, or ashtrays, are witnesses of an ability that deserves to be considered a particularly human one: the ability to stand back from things and look at them from a new perspective. Bottles are not only delivered with a visible label that denotes their contents but also with an invisible one that instructs us as to how bottles should be understood and used. All objects in our environment are furnished with such imperatives and it is mainly in that sense that they condition us. However, with a certain effort that we might call a 'phenomenological' one, we are able to look beyond this invisible imperative and see bottles for what they are, not for what they should be. A bottle which has thus been freed of its value can then be re-evaluated by us, for instance as a candleholder.

"
. . .

Vilém Flusser, *Dinge und Undinge. Phänomenologische Skizzen* (Munich, 1993), p. 17.

creativity. The booty is often made up of broken or incomplete goods, which can only be brought back to life through even more elaborate interventions.

It is arguable whether reusing second-hand objects can be considered NID, or whether this activity should be assigned to the earlier identified area of deliberate repurposing for reasons of creative self-fulfilment. In this particular case, the border seems to be blurred because it is hard to tell by simply looking at the object itself which specific reason might have been the motive for its repurposing. Did that old mortar-sugar bowl come into being because there was no proper sugar bowl at hand or was the mortar specifically acquired for that purpose? If an element of creative handicraft played a role in the act of repurposing, then this particular instance of NID would be rather similar to the activities of the hobbyists, the only difference being that here existing objects instead of semi-finished products are used to create something new. Another significant aspect in this context is an ascetic attitude that implies the deliberate renouncement of consumerism. We differentiate these instances of repurposing from those which occur spontaneously during use.

In the developed, industrial societies this kind of behaviour is mainly found within alternative fringe groups. Their idea of differentiating themselves from a uniform product culture by repurposing individual objects and by favouring any suitable alternative over the products of consumerism is, in other countries, the usual way of life – out of mere necessity. "Initially, with regard to most modern imported goods, the indigenous population usually only had access to those items that were deemed useless and beyond repair by the colonial rulers. Scrap metal and the rubber from car tyres were soon identified and used anew as multi-functional materials. [...] In the developing countries, these materials have never been considered waste. They were seen as useful and recyclable right from the beginning."[125]

However, the following paragraph will show that here, too, not all rubbish is instantly disposed of: One-way or disposable products are only manufactured for one particular purpose and for a single instance of use. We might encounter them, however, in a variety of functions: old soft-drink bottles are painted and used as flower vases, preserving jars with screwtops are not just used to preserve jam, but also as storage containers for either foodstuffs such as coffee, salt, or spices, or for small items such as screws, sewing thread, or similar. Nowadays, there are collection points for old film containers in camera shops, which then forward the containers to nursery schools where they are used as a popular craft material. Empty drink cans might see a second life as an ashtray or a football, and bottles can serve as flower vases, candle holders, watering cans or, when broken, even as a weapon or, along the top of walls, as a deterrent against intruders. Card houses are built with beer mats which are also used as notepads to record the items consumed or, like empty cigarette packs, for exchanging telephone numbers or directions.

But what exactly is the reason why these objects have such an immense potential for changes of use when they were actually intended to be used just once and then discarded? It is exactly because they have already fulfilled their purpose that they are

---

125   Ulrich Giersch and Ulrich Kubisch, *Gummi. Die elastische Faszination* (Berlin, 1995), p. 348 f.

The Plastic Bag

"
...

In the rain, plastic bags are used to protect plaster casts on legs, hairdos, and hats (!), they serve as frost protection for roses, keep the saddles of parked bicycles dry, they are used as a gym bag for trainers, keep food fresh when we go on a trip, serve as a protective mat when we sit on park benches, as a sledge, as a container for carrying water on camping sites, as a watering can, as a red security flag to mark loads that extend beyond the length of a vehicle, as a wind sleeve to indicate the direction and strength of the wind, and so forth.
And let us not forget the folded-up plastic bag kept in the pocket of one's coat for the next impulse purchase. Hence, 'a plastic bag is not one-way packaging.'

"
...

form. Zeitschrift fur Gestaltung, 89 (1980), p. 24 ff.

available to us again and are free to be used differently. Before we throw them away for good, we might just as well use them for a new and different purpose. Free from their initial reason to exist, we can use them however we see fit. And we do not need to feel bad about potentially destroying them through our ulterior uses because the object was destined for the rubbish tip anyway. We do not experience any loss of function or value, the object does not need to be repaired or replaced. On the contrary: By reusing it, we prolong the object's life, we break the cycle of use and disposal, and endow it with a new personal value, which might even save it from the wastebin for good. "This is why we keep used bottles: we transform them and use them for new purposes, for example, as ashtrays. Transformed, empty bottles are witnesses of the continuous transformation of forms, i.e. a method of how humans overcome the given *(das Sein)* in order for it to become what it should be. That is what theory means: not the contemplative gazing at existing forms but an active transformation of preserved forms. And the meaning of life is: the continuous and progressive abolishment and alteration of forms. In other words, the dialectic of theory and practice. And this is commitment: the permanent revolutionary transformation of preserved bottles."[126] Flusser's description of the phenomenon as the meaning of life confirms that the free use of preserved forms is not just a habit but has also become a need.

The process of disposal itself provides some options for NID. Numerous kinds of packaging, such as tins, cups, plastic bags, and cardboard boxes, experience their only post-packaging application as containers for the collection of empty bottles and old paper, as wastebins, or ashtrays. Old cardboard might temporarily be used as a cutting mat for chopping up other cardboard boxes, and old bottles and glass jars are carried to the recycling bin in a plastic bag.

To put it bluntly, one could say that the same behaviour concerning waste objects also becomes apparent in many socially accepted passions for collecting – whether it is about empty perfume bottles, beer bottles, tomato-paste tins, telephone cards, or stamps. All these objects have already fulfilled their original purpose and now, removed from their natural context of use, experience a new form of appreciation or even rise in value. The interaction with these objects changes radically: old stamps are only picked up with tweezers and gloves, and are carefully stored under sheets of parchment in thick albums. At this point, at the latest, they have taken on a new meaning and become unsuitable for any NID application.

Presented at auctions or exhibited in museums, the former disposable products now take centre stage and become interesting again in different respects. Some of these collections might even serve as historico-cultural retrospectives of their original functions and once more connect to the subject of NID. For example, the opening exhibition of Haus Industrieforum Essen *Plastiktüten, Gebrauchskultur im Straßenbild* (The street culture of plastic bags) not only exhibited 450 plastic bags, but also provided a great deal of interesting facts about this item, including related changes of use. Even if these observations cannot be called a proper study, they represent, however, a first attempt at initiating a public debate about this phenomenon.

---

126   Vilém Flusser, *Dinge und Undinge. Phänomenologische Skizzen* (Munich, 1993), p. 25.

Manufacturers often use the additional value of packaging in their advertising strategies to boost the sales of their products. In these cases, potential changes of use are turned into selling points: Yoghurt, for instance, is available in resealable plastic cups suitable for freezing, cakes come in reusable glass baking dishes, and mustard or chocolate mousse are presented in decorated drinking glasses. This approach is successful because, as mentioned earlier, the repurposing of packaging is a fairly common practice anyway and will thus be easily accepted by consumers. The producers of biscuits and sweets offer their goods in specially decorated tins, like, for example, Nürnberger Lebkuchen (gingerbread from Nuremberg), or fudge from Quality Street. The colourful, often embossed tins seem to be too valuable to be thrown away and are used to store all sorts of items.

If the product is targeted at children, the packaging becomes more than just a protective shell to facilitate storage. Games and figures for cutting out can be found on the inside of cardboard packaging, sweets are filled into plastic canes or similar, even the sweets themselves are offered in shapes such as watches or bracelets which can be worn as jewellery before eating. Ferrero advertise their Kinder Eggs not just as sweets but also as a fun surprise and with a toy that is contained in the sweet itself. The egg, wrapped in thin aluminium foil, serves as packaging for an oval plastic egg that contains a toy. The little plastic box can again be used as part of the toy it contains and also as a storage container for other items. Here, the principle of the Russian "Matryoshka" nesting dolls is used to sell chocolate. And furthermore, the strategy of using constantly changing figures and games invokes at the same time a passion for collecting. Nowadays, these stocking fillers are traded amongst enthusiasts at quite steep prices.

In addition to providing ulterior uses with their packaging, companies are also using tokens to appeal to adult collectors. Little pictures that can be peeled out of bottle caps, tokens that have to be cut out of labels and packaging and so on can be kept in bonus booklets, or stuck on collection posters. Depending on the number of tokens, customers then receive a gift to reward them for their loyalty.

These two examples demonstrate that the repurposing of disposable products is a well-known fact and is used strategically in the industry. The phenomenon of repurposing, which has hardly received any attention in scientific studies, has been used quite successfully in the world of consumerism. Although these predefined multiple uses cannot be considered NID, many of these ideas are either copied from, or based on, instances observed in everyday life: a circle or interchange, where changes of use from everyday life serve as inspiration for marketing, and where changes of use predefined by marketing strategists themselves contain new potential for unexpected ways of using things differently.

Multifunctional Products

Multifunctionality has become an established term in the context of design. It signifies an approach where an object is equipped with more than just one function, and where users can choose between the available functions. This strategy has produced kitchen machines that are both mixers and choppers, or waffle irons and toasters, and office furniture that can serve as a table, cabinet, or chair, or, generally, objects that can be transformed and used for one function or another. The all-in-one principle can be applied to every product group on the condition that the product itself is so complex that a spontaneous change of use (i.e. user-initiated multifunctionality) is no longer possible (and/or desired). Under the pretext of multifunctionality, strict and predefined instructions are given for applying the multiple uses of an appliance. There is no intention of providing true freedom of use. On the contrary: A deliberate combination of functions in one object renders it inflexible for individual changes of use. Supposedly space-saving, multifunctional furniture is typically only used in one way and because of their transformational potential these items often require more space than traditional furniture in order to fulfil this function.

It is also hard to ignore the makeshift impression that these pieces tend to convey. A sofabed, for instance, is considered useful if visitors are staying over, but when asking people who use such a sofa as their regular bed it becomes obvious that the sofabed tends to remain in its bed state because people find the daily effort of transformation rather tedious. The state of the room, which has been disfigured by the presence of such a provisional solution, (sofabeds tend to be placed in the middle of the room and need even more space for their covers, cushions, and armrests) is often excused with the standard apology "I haven't got round to making the bed yet." You constantly run into the object that does not usually take up so much space, and the fact that sleeping on this makeshift bed is far less convenient than on a regular one is yet another nuisance.

The example of the sofabed serves to illustrate how difficult it can be to live with these multifunctional pieces of furniture, which raises the question of whether we actually need them at all. After having established that the disadvantages of these items render them almost useless for continuous use, we might just as well fall back on true NID solutions: equipped with a day cover and a few cushions, our normal bed can easily be transformed into a comfortable sitting area, and a good sofa can make a perfect bed for one night, just as it does for an afternoon nap.

In the latter case, even our attitude towards the object is a different, which is to say positive, one. We do not expect perfection when using things differently from their original purpose. On the other hand, we are all the more annoyed about the imperfection of a multifunctional object that we bought specifically because of this feature. While we react with resentment and disappointment in the latter case, we tend to be happy about our ideas and enjoy the flexibility of the objects involved when it comes to NID solutions. We appreciate repurposed things all the more because, in addition to their original function, they deliver added value. Many of our favourite items have attained this status just because of their additional uses, such as our favourite cup, for instance, which we not only use for drinking tea or coffee, but also for drinking juice or water, or for eating muesli or soup.

Modern, all-purpose food processors are a similar case in point. There are just too many disadvantages, which is why they seem to spend their life at the back of the cupboard. Equipped with comprehensive manuals and unidentifiable accessories, these machines tend to confuse their owners, who have to undergo a period of intense study before they might experience any labour saving moment. (This aspect does, of course, not feature in TV advertising spots for these appliances, in which beaming housewives and husbands go about their housework effortlessly by simply pressing a few buttons.) After having properly assembled the appliance, which requires time and space, as well as a power socket, it becomes indeed easier to chop, stir, knead, and grate. However, after the actual job is done the machine has to be disassembled again, each single part needs to be cleaned separately and put away. Any alleged labour-saving in comparison to traditional whisks, graters, or just our plain hands is instantly nullified by a significant increase in additional work during the pre-use and post-use phases. Thus it is hardly surprising that people who own several types of household appliances tend to use the simpler, cheaper ones.

In this context, take a look at the kitchen of a woman we interviewed on this subject: Although she owns a highly complex food processor, she tends to use a simple electrical mixer for making cakes or the like. There is no need for any tedious assembling and disassembling, and even after long periods of disuse it is easy to remember how to use the appliance: there is only one on/off switch with three different speed settings.

On some occasions, however, it seemed to make sense to use the new machine. She recently used it for crushing ice when mixing cocktails, and for mixing lime cordial with rum. But this kind of application was not intended and cost her dearly. Some inaccessible parts inside the technological wonder were clogged by the sugary fluids and made the whole appliance useless. The repurposing of machines like this often ends in a similar fashion, which certainly serves to promote proper and "obedient" use. However, a hammer and towel used to crush ice will not punish their owners for having been misused, and a glass and spoon for making Mojitos will still be perfectly usable in their traditional roles afterwards.

In this context it is worth noting how cleverly industry uses our desire for labour-saving devices in order to sell their complex, expensive, and delicate products. While we are usually perfectly capable of debunking any advertising myth, we are often too gullible when it comes to technology. Men especially, are easily won over by the wonders of technology in the form of gifts for their partners that are meant to compensate for a lack of support with household chores.

To conclude, we can state that multifunctional objects, which pretend to possess some labour-saving potential, are not just unsuitable for changes of use but are also fairly useless in the context of trivial everyday tasks and applications. The consequences of this situation have been aptly summarised by Manfred Sack: "There are utensils that we own but forget about because we do not use them. The work they are supposed to facilitate can be done without them – however badly, imperfectly, or grudgingly."[127] True labour-saving is often achieved more easily through simple and cheap alternatives: a sharp knife, for instance, might save energy several times a day without one having to fall back on technical appliances.

---

127 Manfred Sack, *Alltagssachen. Eine Sammlung von allerlei notwendigen Gebrauchsgegenständen* (Vienna, 1992) p. 68.

In addition to the space-saving and labour-saving principles, there is a third group of multifunctional objects which are relevant in the context of NID: travel products. Travel products are as small as possible, easy to transport and sturdy, and often claim to meet several of our needs at once. There is rainwear that can also double as bag, tent, or bicycle and backpack cover, and there are sets of camping cookware whose lids can also be used as plates or frying pans. But, of course, the prime example is the Swiss Army Knife which will never let you down. This multifunctional tool and its numerous possible applications can save us many an NID effort. We no longer need to turn the tips of knives, or the teeth of keys into screwdrivers. The knife provides a more elegant substitute for breaking bread and making sandwiches with your hands when outdoors (and if necessary you can even clean your teeth afterwards with the integrated toothpick). Depending on the particular model, its owners will be prepared for every eventuality with a handy corkscrew, tin opener, saw, and nail file. In contrast to multifunctional furniture and high-tech kitchen appliances, this all round tool delivers its promises. This is also borne out by the fact that the Swiss Army Knife has become an international sales hit. The potential resentment triggered by some inferior, or hard to operate, elements is easily forgotten when we simply have these things handy when needed. Nor do we find it tedious to constantly carry around all those functional elements that we might not need at all, since the knife tends to endow us with a feeling of omnipotence. The Swiss Army Knife does, however, like most outdoor products, still offer options for ulterior uses such as opening letters with one of its integrated knives, or using the whole object as a paperweight. Besides, "the Swiss Army Knife does feel good in your hand even if there is nothing that needs cutting and you only use it as a hand charm in your pocket."[128]

Having compared the natural multifunctionality of basic forms with the designed multifunctionality of certain products, it seems sensible to extend our concept of what constitutes an object. In this context, Van den Boom has stated: "An object can simultaneously have either one function or another. We will, however, understand this as two separate entities! When one entity is realised, the other is no longer possible."[129] This analysis of the term, which comprises both spontaneous and intentional multifunctionality, is also applicable to this study. We do not need any artificial, additional value in order to recognise an object's multifunctionality because we have the ability to see beyond the original function of things.

Media Products

The last object group that will be analysed is that of media products which, in terms of function, comprise immaterial services. The functionality of these objects cannot be

---

128   Gert Selle, *Siebensachen. Ein Buch über die Dinge* (loc.cit.), p. 216.

129   Holger van den Boom, *Betrifft: Design. Unterwegs zur Designwissenschaft in fünf Gedankengängen* (Braunschweig, 1994), p. 38.

determined by looking at them. They are similar to a black box (often indeed housed in a black plastic casing) which hides their different functions. In terms of the material objects themselves, their suitability for NID is limited to a few examples. These objects are not meant to be repurposed and only rarely meet the necessary preconditions for changes of use.

On the one hand, this is due to the fact that their actual value endows them with a status of preciousness (see the earlier section on disposable products) and, on the other hand, to our not being as familiar and experienced with their form and function as we are, for instance, with those of the more basic shapes. This impedes any potential instances of repurposing. Flusser on this type of appliance: "Some items in my surroundings tend to make me feel uneasy. Be it because I seem to help myself to them, but I actually know that I operate them. Be it because these things are obviously at my disposal and have obviously been put at my disposal, and because I actually dispose of these things without more than a faint idea about their functionality."[130]

The proper operation of these appliances alone demands so much attention and effort that there is no more room left to consider any potential repurposing. "The user becomes a protuberance, an appendix of the appliance, which rules him by doing everything for him and dictating what is still left to be done."[131] The relief that the appliance does what it is supposed to do inhibits any potential thoughts of repurposing. Once the product is switched on and working, it is hard to imagine any change of use. However, once these appliances are switched off or "dead", as it were, it is somewhat easier to do something else with these bulky black boxes that sit in our homes. Then, hi-fi boxes are turned into flower stands or shelves for telephones, lamps, or candleholders. We start to pile and arrange stuff around these high-tech boxes, which can be a bookend one moment and a CD or video tape shelf another. They are themselves piled on top of each other and arranged into technology towers in order to save space. It is a pity, however, that sensitive materials or air vents positioned on the top surfaces of these appliances tend to limit the options for additional uses.

The second NID-relevant aspect in connection with high-tech products, and in particular with the media, are the functions of these appliances, such as their immaterial, intangible services. In the information age we are surrounded by visual and acoustic sources which transmit their news via monitors, light signals, and loudspeakers. When studying the phenomenon of NID in relation to this product group, we must not only focus on the objects themselves, but also on their media-related effects and functions.

Radio and Television

The radio, as an object in its own right, offers few options for repurposing, but different people associate different aspects with its use. Transmitting as it does the human

---

130   Vilém Flusser, *Dinge und Undinge. Phänomenologische Skizzen* (loc.cit.), p. 7.

131   Gert Selle, *Siebensachen. Ein Buch über die Dinge* (loc.cit.), p. 259.

voice, it encourages many people to enter into a dialogue with the appliance. Although there is no "other" who could comment on what is being said, and although these people usually do not tend to soliloquise, the radio seems to encourage people to talk, sing, or dance along. A sense of community, of sharing what is said with other listeners while still being alone and, often, protected in one's private space, seems to evoke this kind of behaviour.

Radios share our most intimate moments and places throughout the day: We listen to them in the morning when we wake up, and they surprise us with whatever is being transmitted at that moment. We listen to them in the bathroom while going through our morning routine, in the kitchen during breakfast, and in the car while driving to work. We know the hosts of our favourite radio programmes personally – or at least we think we do. We dress according to the weather forecast, and the first song we hear will follow us throughout the day. The radio becomes part of our life and we miss it dearly, for instance during a holiday abroad, when we are not able to understand what is going on. On the other hand, it might just be this kind of global transmission of communication that we find alluring: tuning in to broadcasts from other countries can be like going on an acoustic trip around the world. Many people use the radio as a coach when learning a foreign language. The transmission capabilities of the radio, and hence its immaterial NID potential, can, however, reach much farther than that: there are some people who are convinced that, via special frequencies, they can make contact with extraterrestrial beings or even get in touch with the realm of the dead.

Listening to the radio is such a popular activity because it allows us to attend to other business at the same time and this is what renders it so flexible in use. When you ask people why they listen to radios, you will get the obvious answers such as wanting to be informed or to listen to music, but you will also receive some more personal statements: for example in order to stay awake while driving, to spice up monotonous work, to relax after an exhausting day's work, or to take their mind off their own problems. The radio is used for one's own purposes, the programme listened to not actually being of consequence. Radio programmes can provide inspiration for a variety of individual activities. And it is this individual use of what we are listening to that can be considered an NID-related phenomenon.

The short, transitory life of transmitted information has resulted in another form of individual use: With the invention of the tape recorder it became possible to record radio broadcasts. Music can now be mixed and arranged according to one's own taste and without having to go and purchase the relevant songs from a record store. However, this form of pirate copying is not supported by all radio stations. Many radio hosts do not play a whole song through to the end, or talk over it, either in order to identify the origin of the respective copies, or to stop this kind of behaviour altogether.

Due to its straightforward technology, it is easy to build a radio yourself: a coil and a piece of wire will suffice to turn all sorts of things into radios. This is also an interesting aspect in the context of NID. Broadcasting itself is also comparably easy: Even school children are able to create pirate stations by using some simple equipment and free frequencies. However, they must not get themselves caught in the act because, in contrast to the Internet which enables everyone to broadcast themselves, radio frequencies are controlled by the broadcasting corporations and illegal use is considered a crime.

Most of what applies to radio is also true of television. But its far more complex technology makes individual broadcasting without professional help impossible. From the user perspective there are, however, some parallels. Although television usually demands full attention and thus, in comparison to the radio, significantly limits the potential for any additional activities, many people tend to switch on their TV and use it as an acoustic backdrop. Especially for people who live alone this might convey a feeling of not being on their own. They tend to turn their TV on as soon as they get home. Accompanied by the sounds, and every now and again glancing at the monitor, they go about their usual business without really watching any programme in particular.

Regarding content, it is difficult to talk of any repurposing in the NID sense when looking at the use of radio and television. It is, however, interesting that beyond any material changes of use, to which these appliances do not really lend themselves, there is a broad spectrum of possible applications in terms of their media functions. These forms of use were not predefined by developers but have been discovered by users. Virtual space and its related appliances entail a potential for redefinitions of use which we have already analysed in the chapter on new media (page 89).

The Car

In addition to the transmission of information by the media, modern society is shaped by another characteristic that brings the world closer together: The increase in traffic volume, and the development of numerous motorised means of transportation for overcoming distances shape our environment and symbolise maximum mobility. Therefore, as the last example of technological products, we have selected private transport, the motor car. Its fifty-year history as a means of mass transport, its ubiquitous use and presence, suggest that we might discover further changes of use in the context of the car as an object.

Originally designed to transport people and goods, new and individual applications have developed over time. For a long time now the car has been more than a means of getting from A to B. This practical reason has been complemented by emotional and psychological intentions: Today, many people simply go for a drive, savouring the feeling of freedom this activity seems to evoke. Others embark on a tranquil cruise along country roads to calm down after a row or a stressful day. If you look at the gestures and faces of drivers in city traffic or on the motorway, it becomes instantly clear that driving is also used to vent pent-up emotions. Well protected by the privacy of our car and facilitated through speed, these emotions can be let off more easily. Whether other traffic participants are forced to obey to the highway code or whether they are affected by it being infringed: in both cases the car is used to exert power, hence to obstruct others, to overtake them, to take their right of way, and so on. The multiple meanings of these terms suggest that people who lean towards this kind of behaviour – mostly men – do not often have the opportunity (or ability) to fulfil those suppressed desires in any other way.

However, driving is not just used to demonstrate one's virility, it has also become an arena for the battle of the sexes. Almost every female driver or passenger will have come across phrases such as "Frau am Steuer, das wird teuer!" (Woman at the wheel, not a good deal) and "typisch Frau" (woman driver!). Women who, according to male standards, drive well are apparently a rare species that needs special commendation. Most of the time, however, it is nagging and patronising that dominate the female driver/male passenger dialogue. Men are verbally defending one of their last technological bastions. Every woman knows from experience that this type of criticism is usually dished out in a highhanded, whimsical, and unfair manner. Statistically speaking, however, women cause considerably fewer serious accidents than men. This has recently been confirmed once again by a study carried out on behalf of insurance companies.

When the sexes encounter each other in a traffic situation, in particular couples that are sitting in the same car, the car more often than not becomes a *Beziehungskiste* (literally: relationship box)[132], where they will bicker and argue in the most confined space and where just getting out is not an option. If the subject of a gender-specific driving style has been exhausted, then travelling by car offers a plethora of other reasons for picking a fight such as finding the right way and getting one's bearings when reading signs and roadmaps, smoking, or opening windows, and so forth.

In terms of our topic, these observations are relevant as they relate to using cars as a means of exerting power, to threaten others, to start a game of showing off and intimidation by driving dangerously which might even end fatally. Just like radio and television, there is only one predefined function for a car: Driving. How this function is applied, however, depends on the user.

But fighting is not all that happens when the sexes encounter each other in a car. A car, as a movable private space, can also be an ideal love nest. Whenever the home is not available for the exchange of tenderness, the backseat of a car can be a welcome alternative. Here, the car is not used for driving but as a stationary vehicle. The same quality is exploited by open-air cinemas, which usually offer parking spaces with catering which, in winter, are even heated. Similarly, the car is used in prostitution. However, car seats are not just repurposed for sexual intercourse. A car might just as well serve as cheap accommodation when finding a hotel would either be too time-consuming or too expensive.

All these kinds of repurposing are only possible because a car is not simply a vehicle, but also offers an enclosed, lockable space. Wherever we might be, a car will give us a feeling of home, privacy, and intimacy. It is a mobile refuge which, in cities, keeps out noise and strangers, and in the great outdoors protects us from the weather and keeps out wild animals. The same idea is taken up in types of cars such as campervans or mobile

---

132 *Beziehungskiste* is a German slang word for "relationship problem", and the term *Kiste* is also used as a slang word for "car".

1

2

3

4

5

6

1 Car seat as clothes rack
2 Car as sleeping quarters
3 Discarded car tyres as fenders
4 Discarded tractor as playground
5 Delivery van as shop
6 Car tyres as go-karting track barriers

homes. They are essentially the commercial product derived from repurposed mini vans which were, and still are, used as sleeping berths by many globetrotters today.

The Germans' most valued possession offers some further applications: in car races it becomes an accepted sports instrument, or is used for showdowns in illegal road races. With windows everywhere it is an ideal vehicle for sightseeing tours; covered in stickers or painted it becomes a mobile billboard displaying information and advertising, and when parked it can be used for sitting down or for storing things in public spaces. When it comes to crime and violence, the normal function of a car is abolished: it is turned into a murder weapon, is equipped with bombs, or used as a facilitator to commit suicide.

After its useful life as a car we might find it in playgrounds where kids can get a taste of what it means to be at the steering wheel. And all those who do not want to scrap their four-wheeled "mates" completely can at least save some of their parts: car seats are used as fancy chairs in living rooms, hub caps and number plates reappear as wall decoration, and entire carriages are even beheaded and converted into beds.

The various uses and types of repurposing once more demonstrate what we have observed earlier in relation to other much used things: the constant use of cars is accompanied by a variety of new applications which derive from everyday use. Here men are particularly inventive. After all, cars are one of their favourite topics of conversation, take up a lot of their spare time, are an object of identification, and also a status symbol.

In conclusion we can state that NID is present in all product groups, although the form it takes and its frequency might differ. Compared to simple things, cheap or disposable products, which offer a broad spectrum of potential ulterior uses, intentionally designed multi-functional objects tend to prevent such options. With increasing complexity, objects provide fewer opportunities for redefinitions of use. This is particularly true for the "technological wonders" of modern society.

High-tech products take us into a different world of non-intentional use. Activities such as driving a car, or media transmissions such as radio or TV broadcasts can also be used for personal ends. The more the actual type of use is related to immaterial space, the more abstract the act of repurposing becomes. Because if it is not the object itself that is needed and instead it becomes a tool for fulfilling an immaterial need, meaning if it becomes a medium, then the majority of these non-intentional forms of application also belong to the realm of the immaterial. While objects such as televisions and computers offer only limited options for repurposing, watching television or using the computer can entail numerous non-intentional actions. Hence we can say that, depending on the product, the quantity and quality of changes of use are most diversified when we not only consider an object's exterior shape, but also its functions.

Architectural Elements: Walls, Floors, Stairs

We have already noted that in architecture there is little room for Non-Intentional Design because of the degree of planning necessary for the construction of buildings. A different picture emerges, however, when we look at particular elements of architecture, which we will now investigate more closely. An interesting aspect in this context is the fact that houses provide an interface between the inside and the outside, and between private and public space.

In the same way as our interaction with products, we use individual architectural elements in an independent way. But unlike products, architectural elements fulfil their intended function immediately after the production process is completed, thus as soon as the house is built: walls hold the house together, doors let people pass through, windows let in light and fresh air, staircases connect different floors, and floors or ceilings separate them from one another. As stationary elements, and in contrast to products, they are fixed to one particular place. It is, however, exactly this rigid immobility that makes them ideal objects for certain types of applications.

The Wall: Noticeboard and Supporting Structure

We constantly encounter information displayed on walls where it is visible at all times. The different vertical surfaces of houses have developed into special information displays. Doors and certain focal points when entering or leaving rooms are dotted with shopping lists, event reminders, important addresses or phone numbers, or with city maps. Personal items such as collections of photographs and postcards, stickers, and posters are attached to the interior surfaces of doors. Old items can easily be replaced because the wipeable varnish makes it possible to tape things to them. Things that are attached to walls often remain there for longer periods. Even paper that is stuck to a wall with pins will leave traces in the form of a lighter-coloured patch and tiny holes. Nonetheless, we find postcards and wise sayings on the walls of offices or kitchens. In representative rooms, however, there is usually no spontaneous use of walls for personal notes. Here, people tend to decorate their walls in a considered way. Since these wall decorations are usually specifically made for this purpose, they cannot be assigned to the category of NID.

The fact that exterior walls are also suitable for the communication of information has long been known by marketing experts, who use them for large-scale advertising. The walls of underpasses are usually covered with posters, and scaffolding in front of buildings undergoing renovation is often cladded with large sheets bearing advertising messages. If there are not enough suitable surfaces in a city, special billboards are put up, which, in the context of this study, is a good example for the commercial exploitation of a repurposing need. This particular one goes back almost 150 years when advertising pillars appeared in Germany for the first time. However, alongside commercial messages we can find personal notes everywhere in public spaces, such as on wastebins, lampposts, or the like.

Electrical distribution boxes get covered
with advertising.

In private spaces we also find noticeboards, a term that still points to the object's origin. Information fixed to a wall is visible for everyone who walks past it. Besides this type of repurposing, walls are also ideally suited for parking things (such as bicycles) or leaning things against (such as ironing boards and clothes-horses). Some commercial products use the principle of "leaning against a wall" and so need fewer legs or static elements. What was considered avantgarde design in the 1980s, is today even available at IKEA, where you can find shelves and lamps which are stabilised by simply leaning against a wall. Walls also offer us a backrest when sitting, or a support when standing, children practice their handstands against walls, and women use them to stretch the muscles of their legs. Walls do not just carry the weight of the house, we also use them as a support either for ourselves or for other objects.

The second type of wall surface suitable for repurposing is the window. Windows can be used to display goods laid out inside to the world outside. Today, shop windows are such an inherent part of shopping areas and malls that we cannot consider them to be NID in the context of traditional windows. However, in private homes windows are also used for interior or exterior decoration. When children paint colourful images on them, or, during the Christmas season, decorate them with stars, the glass of the window takes on a different meaning. This hole in the wall that originally was meant to let in light and fresh air now becomes a special wall of light, which is used for decoration, or, using daylight that shines on them, can help with tracing patterns, or can replace expensive light tables when looking at slides.

The Floor: Interior and Exterior Seating Alternative

Standing and walking on the floor is normal, sitting on it, however, is fairly rare in our culture. People do not want to get dirty and generally prefer to sit more comfortably. Nonetheless, interior and exterior floors are often used as alternative seating. Young people, especially, appreciate this casual way of sitting. To the grief of many a parent, homework is done while sitting on the floor, and young girls often hold tea parties sitting on carpets. Even whole dinner parties are often celebrated in this way because there are simply not enough chairs for every guest to go round. A tabletop propped up on cardboard boxes then becomes a dinner table that can easily seat ten people.

Outside we do not just find people sitting on the lawn but, on a warm summer day, whole schoolyards are turned into parks and it becomes difficult to lure the pupils back inside again. Some lessons are then held outside and the schoolyard becomes a classroom.

The Stairs: A Place for Sitting, Playing, and Sports

We usually find stairs more comfortable for sitting on than the plain ground. How natural it is for us to take place on stairs can be observed not only at such popular places as the Spanish Stairs in Rome, or at Cologne Cathedral. Ancient Greek theatre already

2

1　The floor as a natural seating for children
2　...for adults, however, it takes a little
　　getting used to
3　Stairs as a place for eating and sitting

exploited the principle of seat-stairs arranged in circles in order to save space and provide a good view of the stage.

Skateboard, mountain bike, and rollerblade enthusiasts, too, have discovered the rhythmical up and down of public stairs and use these structures to demonstrate their skills. Arguably, a more impressive way to spend your free time than using carpeted staircases as slides.

If the staircase inside the house cannot be avoided, then it often becomes a popular place for leaving notes and messages, and the rather tiring up and down can lead to our leaving items at the top or bottom of the stairs until we have to go in the appropriate direction again.

The list of possible ways to repurpose architectural elements is endless. Compared to other NIDs, their original function is not compromised. Most objects only attain their function through human activity. Architectural elements, however, are self-contained. They also fulfill their purpose without any active human involvement. We do not need to do anything for the walls to carry weight, for the floor to be flat, and for the windows to let in light. These elements are only used actively when we start repurposing them. Only then do we see them as things and *a wall* becomes *the wall* with which we develop a personal relationship. Through these changes of use that go beyond architectural functions we liberate walls, floors, and stairs from their otherwise anonymous existence.

We deal with architectural elements in the same way as we deal with basic forms to which we assign several functions that are used alongside each other. Architectural elements have also been around for such a long time that certain changes of use, such as sitting on stairs, have become established. We can, however, clearly observe a difference between changes of use in private and public spaces: a lamppost, for instance, transforms itself into a bicycle stand, a billboard, and a supporting structure – a multifunctionality that cannot be achieved by a floor lamp in the living room. The wall that is decorated with pictures on the inside, is disfigured with graffiti on the outside, and used as a urinal. At home, floors are clean and shiny, and we might even take our shoes off before walking on them, whereas in public spaces the ground is used as a wastebin or ashtray where we leave our rubbish or cigarette butts. Not only does the shift from private property to communal property result in numerous forms of repurposing which are used by many people but, sometimes, also in a more careless, if not destructive, treatment of things.

The Process
of Discovery

Product Characteristics: Form, Material, Value, and Availability

After having looked at certain object groups and places in which changes of use occur, and after having arrived at the conclusion that the phenomenon of NID permeates all areas of our everyday life as an ability that is applied to everything everywhere, we will now analyse more carefully the process that leads to the creation of Non-Intentional Designs. As we already pointed out earlier, the ability to associate plays a crucial role in the context of NID, as it enables us to separate an object's characteristics from its functionality so that we can use it for non-intentional purposes. Form and material are among the primary characteristics that we use as a basis for evaluating a potential NID implementation.

The pointed form of a needle, for instance, opens up a plethora of potential applications. In particular the characteristic of being able to perforate something very finely opens up a multitude of options: apart from sewing up pieces of cloth, needles are used to fix posters to walls, to remove splinters from under the skin, to pierce ears, or to clean shower heads. The actual form or shape is usually the first selection criterion that we define in order to find a suitable NID. Often, however, there are several products that have the same shape. If we are looking for receptacles, for instance, we could use glasses, cups, mugs, tins and bowls. Once we have made a decision regarding volume and contents, there are still quite a number of receptacles left that we could use. Therefore, the criterion of form alone is not sufficient for finding the object that will be best suited to a particular instance of repurposing. Further characteristics have to be considered in order to select the "ideal" NID.

The material qualities of an object are also very important: Although jam jars and yoghurt pots have a similar shape, the former are actually used far more frequently in the context of NID when they are retained as storage devices. The reason for this is that glass as a material is generally considered more valuable in terms of look and feel, it has greater density, and does not fall over easily. If a glass is filled it is still possible to see its contents, which can be useful when storing spices. Its smooth surface allows it to be cleaned properly and since glass is also watertight, its contents are well protected from damp, or can even be liquid themselves. The material qualities of glass and an efficient closing mechanism make the jam jar better suited for repurposing than other, similar containers made from different materials.

However, even after having narrowed down options on the basis of form and material, several alternatives might still remain: A drinking glass and a mustard jar, for instance, display almost identical shapes and material characteristics. Still, the cheaper mustard jar is generally the first choice when it comes to storing children's paintbrushes in case some residual paint makes it unusable later.

Hence secondary characteristics such as value and dispensability form the third criterion on which NID applications are based. If an instance of repurposing might potentially damage an object, we will prefer to use cheap or disposable products, for example for mixing paint or for cleaning paint brushes. A beaker for toothbrushes, on the other hand, must also meet some visual criteria since it is "on show" and therefore we will generally give preference to a higher-quality glass container for this purpose.

However, we do not always have at our disposal such a rich spectrum of options. In a hotel room, for instance, we will quite happily use a plastic cup, originally intended for rinsing out our mouth after brushing our teeth, to drink the wine we have bought during our holiday. We do not do this because we think that the plastic cup is particularly well suited for this purpose but because there is no other object at hand that could fulfil this task. Hence, the availability of objects is the fourth and last criterion by which we narrow down options and arrive at a particular NID solution. After having defined which particular characteristics the object in question must have, it is eventually an object's availability that determines whether it will be used in an NID context.

The following rule can be applied to instances of NID: The higher the number of object attributes that are consistent with our needs, the more positive we consider the resulting repurposing solution to be.

The Time Factor: Finding a Solution and Permanent Changes of Use

In addition to the characteristics of an object, the time we have to find a solution is crucial when selecting a particular NID. A typical factor for the creation of NIDs is the need to find an instant solution to a problem. Usually, instances of NID occur when we do not have the time to procure the missing, original item and need an immediate substitute. In these situations, towels are used to mop up water puddles in the bathroom or the kitchen, knives are turned into hammers or screwdrivers, letters are opened with keys, and T-shirts are used to clean spectacles. Spontaneity and time pressure are important criteria for the creation of many NIDs.

On the other hand, there are deficiencies that do not call for an immediate solution. Many non-intentional applications in the domestic sphere are the result of a permanent search for solutions until we eventually come up with a suitable idea. Shelves made from cardboard boxes, wooden boards, or bricks, slat frames made from Europallets, lamp shades created using old cartwheels or flower pots: all these examples represent changes of use that did not occur spontaneously but were planned; they are the result of a match between our search pattern and a particular object. The process taking place in the back of our mind follows the same principle as the one employed during instantaneous cases of repurposing: we are looking for objects that match our solution matrix, be it an immediately accessible device for cleaning glasses or a cheap alternative to traditional furniture. We are always looking for particular characteristics and functions that an object must possess.

Apparently, the lifespan of NIDs seems to grow in proportion to the time we have available for finding a solution. The more time we invest in finding a solution, the more durable this solution will be. An increase in the time available for solving a problem results in equally higher expectations concerning the result. We expect the repurposed object to fulfil the new function more or less perfectly.

Another reason for permanent changes of use is established when the spontaneously selected object fulfils its new task satisfactorily, so that there is no longer the need to acquire a new product. In these cases, it is not due to planning but the result of our positive experiences with the repurposed object that the solution becomes permanent. This is why slat frames made from Euro-pallets and mugs as containers for pens are successful as permanent NID applications.

Reversibility: Returning to the Original State

When trying to analyse the durability of NIDs, we have to consider the aspect of reversibility in the sense of restoring original functions. The question as to whether, and how radically, a product has to be changed for a new purpose, which might imply the product's becoming useless for its original function, is another significant selection criterion and defines the durability of a NID application. In order to shed more light on this aspect, we will briefly summarise the different time and change-related phases of NIDs.

We need to differentiate between things that are only repurposed for a short period of time and those that are repurposed permanently. The former are not usually changed in terms of shape or material, while the latter have to be divided into those that, after having been repurposed, can no longer revert to their original function, and those that can do so. Examples of domestic objects whose function is changed temporarily while they maintain their original role are chairs or ladders that are briefly used as shelves or clothes racks, or books that are used for smoothing paper or for pressing flowers.

In the public domain, most changes of use are temporary because it is an area of transit which is used by many and a permanent change of use implemented by one person might be disadvantageous for others. In public areas, most instances of repurposing occur in connection with finding somewhere to sit. Fences, steps, or flower containers are used as seats but their original function is not permanently compromised. So we can say that there are a number of existing objects in private as well as in public areas that lend themselves to temporary changes of use without any need for radical alterations.

Permanent changes of use that could, in theory, be reversed because the original function has not been destroyed, are predominantly found in the domestic area. Examples in this context are the drinking glass used as a beaker for toothbrushes and the biscuit tin turned storage container for letters. Since, in these cases, the products can no longer be used in their original function as long as they have to fulfil their new purpose, we first have to make sure that we can do without them for the period of repurposing.

Irreversible, permanent changes of use mostly occur in connection with relatively cheap objects at home, in the garden, or at work. Examples in this context are: varnish stored in a jam jar, a jam jar with a hole in its lid for screws, or a cut-up plastic bottle used as a wasp trap. Such objects are only useful for these types of NIDs if we do not need, or want, to use them any more for their original purposes. In public spaces, however, destruction brought about by repurposing is considered an offence under the vandalism act.

An Example: Rain Protection without Umbrellas

Our strategies for finding NIDs and making a virtue out of necessity are diverse and not focused on one particular object. Flexible, not rigid, thinking in the context of dealing with things is the basis for applications of repurposing. A number of factors are important when it comes to NID solutions: qualities of shape and material, value and availability, the time available for finding a solution, and the possibility of returning the object to its original state. We will illustrate these aspects using the example of a typical NID application:

If it is raining and there is no umbrella to hand, we look for alternatives to cover our heads and clothes and protect them from getting wet. In our mind, we create a list of characteristics that the makeshift solution must have:

- watertight or water resistant, at least for the period of intended use
- thin and covering a large area for an almost complete body coverage
- light, so that the we do not get tired too quickly when the material is draped over head and body
- instant availability

In order to complement these abstract features, our brain compares a number of instances of repurposing that used to meet the required specifications such as:

- jackets wrapped over the head
- unfolded newspapers
- plastic bags
- other bags

If the rain surprises us while we are out on the streets, the possibilities of suitable items for protection are limited. Further considerations, such as whether the wet conditions will destroy our temporary means of protection, hence ruin the fabric of our jacket, or turn an as yet unread newspaper into mush, will be crucial for our decision making.

Things are slightly different if we had already planned to walk in the rain without an umbrella before leaving the house. In this case, there is more time to come up with ideas about how we can manage to stay dry. Additionally, there is a larger choice of objects at home which can serve as a temporary rain protection.

Depending on the situation, we will then choose an available object that best matches our criteria. And if there is no suitable item at all, we still have the option of hiding under a roof and waiting for the rain to let up. Alternatively, we can sprint from one canopy to the next in order to reduce the wet intervals as much as possible. Popular rain protection areas, that is NID alternatives to a repurposed and portable item, are trees, awnings, roofed galleries, protrusions on walls, house entrances, and bus stops.

3

1 Roof as rain protection
2 Baseball cap as rain protection
3 Roof as rain protection

Personality: Pro or Contra Types

If we look at the above solutions, it becomes obvious that there are only very few analogies apart from the fact that they all serve as protection from rain. Whether we decide on a repurposing solution, and if so for which one, largely depends on our personality. Some men may find it embarrassing to present themselves in public with a plastic bag or newspaper over their heads and therefore prefer getting their hair wet while running through the rain. Under no circumstances, however, would some women risk ruining their hairdo and therefore happily make do without the jacket that was initially put on to protect them from wind and cold.

There are also differences in terms of personal creativity and individual evaluations of NID solutions. While some can see a coat rack in a simple nail on the wall, a chair in the hall, or a handle of the utility room, others are either unable to come up with these solutions or consider them to be too much of a compromise to be acceptable.

Moving into a new home also represents a very informative area for our investigation. For some people, the unfinished condition of the new living space and the related stopgap solutions regarding furniture and fixings are simply part of the experience. The interior is completed as a running process. Others, however, have planned everything in advance and move into a fully furnished house or flat that leaves little room for any NIDs. Living with, and using, NIDs is experienced and evaluated very differently and depends on personality, upbringing, social and cultural environment. These factors influence the use of NIDs and define whether we experience them as practical solutions or as rather annoying and temporary means to an end.

Non-Intentional Design in Public Spaces

While the home represents a private space for individuals and families, the public sphere is shared by everyone and needs to accommodate a multitude of needs.

Hannah Arendt, whose political theories emphasise the significance of the public realm for a functioning society, states that public space creates both community and identity by simultaneously separating and connecting people.[133] Each individual object in this space must fulfil the same function as the space itself: objects in the public space play a significant role in helping people to overcome the subjectivity of their private sphere, by offering themselves as projection screens for people's differing perceptions. They initiate interaction by allowing for a multitude of perspectives. We want to take up this thought and extend it by claiming that these objects also allow for a variety of different uses.

Objects exist in public, as well as in private, spaces. The question is whether objects are used differently in these two spheres. In both public and private spaces, we can observe a discrepancy between intended use as defined by designers and actual use by users. Objects in private and public spaces display different characteristics, and consequently there is also a difference in people's behaviour. We can thus assume that there are also differences in changes of use depending on whether objects are located in exterior or interior spaces. The majority of things that surround us at home were deliberately chosen to meet a particular need. The objects we encounter outside our homes often are what their name implies: objectionable. They are either not used at all, they get in our way, or they do not meet our personal aesthetic, emotional, or functional expectations. Since we use the things we have chosen to live with at home in many non-intended ways, it seems fair to assume that the same behaviour occurs in public spaces because they are full of objects that can hardly fulfil every person's needs – although we all must live with these things as soon as we enter public spaces.

Designed Environments

Everyday redesign through use is not bound to a particular place, it happens everywhere where people and things come together. Repurposing in the public sphere happens when existing objects are used in a way that was not intended by the public authorities. Objects in public spaces, such as residential buildings, offices, museums, schools, streets, bridges, underground car parks, and parks, as well as wastebins, recycling containers, street signs, lampposts, banisters, fences, benches, flower containers, and ultimately spaces themselves are designed professionally to enable interaction and organise communal life. Various disciplines such as architecture, design, and urban planning are involved in tackling related problems. During the development of public design projects a variety of interests must be considered that might, in parts, contradict each other. City dwellers are not a homogenous group of people: there are young and old people, women and men, different income groups and people from different

---

133   Cf. Hannah Arendt, *Vita activa oder vom tätigen Leben* (Munich, 1967).

cultural backgrounds. Different needs have to be catered for at different times of the day or in different city districts. For example, a working mother needs efficient transport from her home to her workplace in the morning, a playground for the children in the afternoon, and a theatre or cinema in the evening.

In addition to urban-planning departments, retailers are increasingly participating in the design of public spaces by presenting their goods not just in the shops but also on the streets, and by putting up all sorts of signs. Restaurants mark their territory on the pavement with flower containers, parasols or fences. Small businesses also exert an increasing influence on issues related to street furniture. In Cologne, for example, the retailers located in the vicinity of the Cathedral have formed an interest group which has had some success in demanding that the square around the *Dom* should be made unattractive for skaters, street artists, and homeless people.

Urban Passengers

What role do citizens play in the designed environment? Do they only use it, or do they actually co-design public space? We believe that people actively participate by redesigning, or repurposing, objects and structures in public spaces. Two examples serve to demonstrate this point: An announcement for the next meeting of an action group is fixed to a wastebin, which was set up for the disposal of rubbish. Here, the wastebin is not used for collecting rubbish but for displaying information. Further common examples are stairs or flower containers used as seats when their original purpose was to overcome differences in height or to green the city. In both cases people interfere with the design of public spaces by using an existing infrastructure for their own, non-intended, purposes.

Objects in Public Spaces

Urban planning departments have the task of organising the complex structure of cities. They have to find solutions that match people's expectations about public spaces and the objects found there. Most of these objects are immobile and fixed to a particular place, either because they are too heavy to be moved, such as flower containers for instance, or because they are fixed to the ground in order to prevent theft or repositioning. The language of urban planners nonetheless refers to these objects as "furniture", thus alluding to items such as sofas, chairs, tables, and cabinets that are used to furnish our homes. These objects are indeed strikingly similar to those we find in interior spaces: the counterpart to the sofa is the bench, wastebins and flower containers can also be found at home, and lighting similar to floor lamps and pendants also exists in public spaces. There are even cabinets such as distribution boxes (which are locked and therefore only accessible to certain people). And last but not least there are newspaper boxes, vending machines for cigarettes and sweets which can be used by anyone for a small sum of money.

The construction and appearance of street furniture, however, is much sturdier than that of its domestic counterparts.

It would certainly be possible to design public city spaces in a better way than is the case in most German cities. The rapid and, in parts, inconsiderate reconstruction after the Second World War has also contributed to compromising user-friendly urban planning. Surprisingly, however, these cities function nonetheless. Locals as well as tourists use these public spaces and the communal infrastructure without disassembling them or replacing things with their own designs. It is a worthwhile exercise to try and imagine what would happen if everybody were allowed to design public spaces according to their personal preferences. These spaces are, after all, areas for living, just like our homes. This kind of intervention is, of course, not allowed, or at best controlled and limited to particular places and times. If no official permission was granted for painting walls, this activity is considered vandalism.

Similarly, placing private furniture in public spaces is only permitted when it is bulky refuse to be collected by the council.

Apart from a few exceptions, people do not seem to object to having their activities and creativity regulated by laws. Why? As mentioned earlier, our basic premise is that each designed object entails possibilities of use that are different from those intended. In this context, an object's aesthetic quality is of no importance. For most people, this openness for interpretation seems to provide sufficient possibilities for an active participation in an object's design. It is, however, equally obvious that professional design has not yet sufficiently exploited its own ability to create objects for the public sphere which are deliberately designed to allow for multiple uses.

Private Objects and Communal Goods

Objects which are used and repurposed in public spaces can be divided into two groups: those that were placed there in order to fulfil a particular purpose and those that are meant to beautify the environment. They are city furniture and are therefore considered public property. However, private items are used outside the home as well. People carry or push around personal items such as umbrellas, prams, and bicycles. Prams can be used to carry heavy shopping items and umbrellas can serve as canes. Both objects are also used during the carnival season, when beer barrels are transported through the city in prams and umbrellas are used for catching sweets that are thrown from the floats or as protection against being hit by them.

In this chapter, however, we will mainly focus on the repurposing of "furniture" found in public spaces; flower containers, parking meters, lampposts, street signs, wastebins, benches, billboards, advertising columns, telephone booths, and so on.

Repurposing: Sitting, Informing, Securing

"Street furniture" is predominantly repurposed for sitting, distributing printed or handwritten information, and parking bicycles. For each of these three activities there are specially designed objects such as benches, billboards, and bicycle stands. However, there do not seem to be enough of them around, or they might be badly designed so that people prefer to use alternatives instead. In the following passage we will introduce these alternatives grouped according to the above-mentioned three activities.

Sitting

Sitting in public spaces can be considered an activity by which someone clearly demonstrates, more clearly at least than by walking or driving, that they intend to stay for some time. The purpose of walking and driving is to get from one place to another. In these cases, the public space is a passageway, or a space of transit. When walking becomes ambling, that is when speed is reduced and we walk along the same route several times, then the street can become an arena for presentation. There are different reasons why we might decide to sit down in public spaces: often we are simply tired and need a rest, or we appreciate a particular view or situation, we enjoy the sunshine, or we might be waiting for someone. Often we sit down in groups in order to communicate. And, of course, there is the popular activity of sitting down outside restaurants or cafés to eat or drink something. (We will, however, exclude the latter because they represent private businesses.)

Urban-planning departments put up benches at those places that, on the basis of empirical studies or plain common sense, are considered popular spots for taking a rest. Benches can often be found in parks or in environments that provide beautiful views, and in places where people have to spend some time waiting, for example, at bus or tram stops. Sometimes, however, you can see benches that look as though someone had simply abandoned them there. We could not help but think that this was the case with a bench we came across during our research. This bench had been positioned in such a way that, after having crossed a dual carriageway, you could sit down, marvel at the beauty of the traffic and contemplate the question as to whether you would ever be able to get back to the other side in one piece.

There are also spaces in cities where sitting is deliberately made difficult: These are usually places where homeless people, drug users, or youths hang around for longer periods of time, for instance around train stations. If there happen to be any benches at all they are designed in such a way that it is impossible to lie on them. In these areas, but also in others where there are benches, many people use other objects for sitting such as stairs, flower containers, barriers, or distribution boxes. It is unlikely that people are unaware of the original function of these objects, because things in public spaces tend to have a low complexity. Everyone is perfectly able to tell the difference between a flower container and a bench, wich means the reason for changes of use is not an insufficient indication function.

3

In situations that entail waiting, people look for somewhere to sit down, as here, waiting for the Weser ferry:

1 Waste skip as seating

2 Bollard as seating

3 Anchor as seating

We believe that there are two reasons why people sit on objects that are not meant to be used that way: firstly, there might indeed be a lack of dedicated seating and the need to sit down often overcomes us when there is no appropriate furniture around. Secondly, there is the earlier-mentioned ability of designed objects to allow for different uses, or, to put it differently, there is our ability to recognise several potential uses in a designed object. What all those objects that are temporarily used as seating have in common is a certain height – similar to that of regular seating furniture – stability, and cleanness.

Most barriers are of a convenient height for sitting on since they are designed in relation to human proportions in order to prevent us from either slipping through below or climbing over, them. We can also assume that barriers are usually sturdy because otherwise they would not fulfil their purpose in the first place. They might often be somewhat lower and more uncomfortable than proper seating furniture, but because they have a smaller surface area they are also less prone to collecting dirt. If they are not too low, then we can also work on the assumption that no dog has lifted its leg at them. Conveniently enough, barriers can often be found at exactly those places where setting up benches was deliberately avoided.

At Cologne's central Neumarkt area the absence of benches and the presence of barriers, for instance, can be explained by the fact that this is a meeting place for junkies and dealers. However, Neumarkt is also a central tourist area and therefore the city administration tries to keep the drug scene at bay by strategic non-design. It is a perfect place to observe how barriers around trees perfectly fulfil their purpose as options for sitting.

Many flower pots and containers also have an ideal sitting height and are hence used as temporary seats. However, this particular "furniture" has one significant drawback: it is rarely clean. The soil necessary for the growing of plants can often be found on the edges of the containers as well. Some people also use flower containers as wastebins. Nonetheless these containers are relatively often used as benches, especially in areas that are well looked after, such as pedestrian zones.

Stairs provide an almost perfect option for sitting on, in particular for larger groups – think, for example, of the Spanish Stairs in Rome. Thanks to the different heights of the individual steps, stairs allow for a variety of group arrangements; they are also sturdy and relatively clean.

2

4

Resting and Sleeping in the Open:

1 Park bench as bed
2 Workbench as bed
3 Pushbike as bed
4 The roof of Milan Cathedral as bed

Providing Information

In public spaces information is primarily distributed by means of posters and hand-written notes where people offer, or search for, goods or services, people or pets. Announcements and graffiti also belong to this group. There are billboards and advertising columns for putting up posters, but they are only used commercially. For most people the price of renting this kind of advertising space would be totally disproportionate to the benefits they hope to gain through the dissemination of their message. The intended use of these surfaces is therefore beyond the means of most people. What, then, are the alternatives?

There are different alternatives, depending on whether the information is sprayed onto a wall, or written on a piece of paper. Spraying in general, and in particular graffiti, is considered a criminal offence, especially if private property is involved; for example, the wall of a house, or a train carriage. These acts are often irreversible, or at least hard to reverse, and therefore urban councils try to prevent them. Many city councils or transport organisations even offer rewards to those who denounce the sprayers. We can therefore assume that someone who applies graffiti to public or private property is aware of committing a criminal offence. Since creating graffiti is risky and removing them is resource-intensive, and because the creators consider their works to be pieces of art, we can conclude that equally valuable surfaces are selected in order to honour the effort that went into the project. In short: The act as such is so meaningful that the surface used needs to be equally valuable.

On the other hand, people who use notes or posters to distribute their information, needs, or announcements prefer recycling containers, lampposts or poles, and public wastebins – depending on the size of the information-carrying material. Less popular are distribution boxes (possibly because it is forbidden to attach any private notes or posters) and any private property such as letterboxes, telephone booths, or newspaper containers. The fact that you rarely find notes on these items is probably due to their being removed on a regular basis.

Cars, which in principle would be well suited for the application of notes and posters, are not used at all, since it can be assumed that the owner (who would then also be the recipient of the message) is not very likely to take this kindly. It is, however, quite common nowadays to stick adverts behind windscreen wipers.

The result of this analysis is that people tend to go for negative selection: each smooth surface, the defacing of which is not explicitly forbidden, can be used for distributing personal information.

2

3

1 Lamppost as notice board
2 Street sign as sticker board
3 Windscreen wiper as holder for parking
   fines
4 Windscreen wiper as holder for flyers

Securing Bicycles

Special pieces of street furniture also exist for bicycles: bicycle stands. There are different models, for instance some only allow for locking the bicycle at the front wheel while with others the bicycle must be jacked up or hooked up. Simpler models allow for several different positions and the more complex ones usually only for one.

With the increasing number of new bicycle models which can be quite valuable, and the corresponding rise in cases of bicycle theft, bicycle stands have become more complex. A few years ago they were still comparably inconspicuous and sometimes could hardly be differentiated from bollards. Today, they tend to be larger structures, some of them even bearing advertising boards on top. These objects could be seen as a form of Non-Intentional Design which has been commercialised.

However, many cyclists do not leave their bicycles in these stands, probably because the stands are often dysfunctional. Their weaknesses have already been indicated above. Additionally, there is sometimes a risk of bending the front wheel, or there is no way to lock both frame and wheel. The fact that these stands are not used as much as one would expect can be attributed to bad design.

Public spaces, however, offer enough alternatives for locking up bicycles. Most popular are, again, barriers, but also street signs, traffic lights, lampposts, and parking meters – therefore all vertically arranged bars or poles of adequate height.

3

4

1 The railings of an underground station
   as bicycle stand
2 Palm tree as bicycle stand
3 Tree barrier as bicycle stand
4 Street sign support as bicycle stand

Constructive and Destructive Repurposing

Repurposing in public spaces is not always a constructive act. In destructive acts of repurposing objects are either destroyed or given a personal mark. Unlike in private spaces, where people can do as they please, this kind of behaviour in public spaces is considered a criminal offence. Constructive repurposing endows objects with additional uses which might temporarily obstruct their original purpose but will never annihilate it. In addition to the examples listed above, pavement painting, and the decoration of tree stumps with flowers or garden gnomes also belong to this category. A rather charming example we came across on Cologne's Aachener Straße consisted of a steel tube with a diameter of about the same as a pole for street signs. Someone must have taken pity on its all too obvious uselessness and given its life new meaning by using the tube as a Christmas-tree stand. The tree adorned the street for quite some time.

We also attribute so-called acts of vandalism to the category of destructive repurposing if these acts annihilate the original purpose of an object. Urinating against public buildings or greenery, which makes it temporarily impossible for other people to stay in the same area and which can result in damage to brickwork or plants, would be another example. There are two types of objects in public spaces that are popular targets for destruction: objects which seem to be dispensable or whose purpose is not understood, and authoritarian objects which only allow for one prescribed kind of use. Works of fine art are an example for the first type. These pieces are often painted on, or interfered with in such a way that a feeling of aggression is clearly visible. Presumably these objects do not mean anything to the people who commit these acts and therefore seem redundant to them. This rejection is expressed through destruction. Examples of authoritarian design, which also tends to be rejected, would be benches with separate seats which allow only for one sitting position and not, for example, for lying on, as well as wastebins whose opening is so small that it only takes objects of a certain size. There is certainly a good reason for both of these design approaches. Homeless people are meant to be prevented from sleeping on the benches, and the disposal of domestic rubbish in public wastebins in order to save money is also meant to be prevented. Authoritarian solutions, however, tend to evoke antagonism.

Appropriation

The desire to appropriate an object is certainly one of the reasons for such idiosyncratic instances of repurposing. The need to put one's stamp on objects predominantly arises when dealing with industrially produced consumer goods. Similarly, in public spaces where many people use the same objects, a desire to appropriate public property through individual use might emerge.

By interpreting objects and their use in an individual way, people prove to themselves and others that they are able to exert influence over that space, that they participate in its design. The more eye-catching and permanent these acts of repurposing are, the stronger the desire for appropriation might have been. This becomes

2

4

Exterior wall as canvas for graffiti
Shop blinds as canvas for graffiti
Electrical distribution boxes as canvas
for graffiti
Garage door as canvas for graffiti

obvious when observing the behaviour of teenagers in public. The most significant interventions in public spaces, often bordering on destruction, are carried out by young people.

Self-Determination

Urban public spaces do not offer much freedom for the individual. Almost everything is regulated and prescribed: areas that can be used for parking cars or bicycles, paths one can take and so forth are all predetermined. In this context, idiosyncratic use is an expression of personal freedom and rebellion against rules and regulations.

A conscious or sub-conscious negation of predetermined rules of behaviour demonstrates independence which, similar to appropriation, is easier to realise in one's own home than in public. Nonetheless, people seem to look for occasions that allow for independent behaviour in public without disturbing others. One example for this gentle form of rebellion is when people ignore predefined, paved routes, and find their own ways. These often turn into dirt tracks clearly marking the route preferred by most people. A suggestion brought forward by some clever urban planners, who wanted to hold back on the implementation of fixed routes through newly constructed areas and instead wait for these dirt tracks to appear first, is a good example for the meaningful integration of non-intended uses into professional design processes.

Obviously, repurposing of objects is also an everyday occurrence in public space. Constructive and reversible types of repurposing public property, as opposed to destructive and irreversible ones, are clearly the more desirable option for both city budgets and citizens. Those responsible for the design of public spaces should think about how the objects in these spaces can be endowed with additional functions, instead of lending themselves as targets for violent acts.

Public Man – Private Woman?

The separation of our environment into public and private areas has been a constant subject of discussion in urban planning, architecture, and sociology, with public space being of particular interest regarding its use by different groups of the population. The frequency and types of behaviour in public space are considered indicators for how people feel in, and about, those spaces and therefore for whether a city as a system is actually working. A fundamental function of this system is communication with strangers. "The city demands that we deal with the 'other'. It is a constitutional condition for the political and social subject. In this, the city teaches us to be tolerant and thus represents the civilising degree of urbanity."[134]

Operating in urban public environments is the archetypical form of communal life and therefore also a fundamental condition for public politics and media. The Greek term for city, *polis*, also points to the close relationship between city and politics.

Historically, the home has been the domain of women, and to a large degree this is still true today. On average, women spend more time at home and therefore assume greater responsibility for its design. In contrast, public spaces used to be the exclusive domain of men where women were excluded. In some countries this is still the case today, and even in Germany, we can still observe a tendency towards male dominance in public spaces. The gender-specific separation between private and public life, and the related juxtaposition of family and society, represents a concept from the 19th century. Feminist sociologists criticise the assumption of this concept as a "timeless universal"[135] because it leads to a rigidification of traditional attributions, and makes it harder for women to gain access to public life, and thus to politics.[136]

How ingrained this spatial separation of the genders still is up to this day is evident in the fact that the majority of those responsible for the design of public spaces are men. Professions that deal with the design of public spaces, such as architecture and urban planning, are mostly staffed by men. So we can say that men have a far greater say in the planning and designing of public space. Whereas men used to design these spaces for themselves, the (alleged) interests of women are also taken into account today.

The better part of urban design, however, still originates from an era when men were the predominant users of this space. And nowadays it is still questionable whether the current (male) planners are at all able to understand women's needs. We cannot help but think that for the majority of the constantly increasing number of women in public life, existing urban designs tend to be useless, and therefore women have taken to repurposing them for their own needs. We therefore assume that the majority of changes of use in public spaces are implemented by women, not by men. This is also

---

134   Frank Herterich, 'Urbanität und städtische Öffentlichkeit', in *Die Materialität des Städtischen*, ed. Walter Prigge (Basel, Boston, 1987), p. 218.

135   Karin Hausen, 'Öffentlichkeit und Privatheit', in *Journal für Geschichte*, vol.1, (1989), p. 23.

136   Cf: Gabriele Köhler, 'Städtische Öffentlichkeit und Stadtkultur', in *Stadt-Land-Frau, Soziologische Analysen, feministische Planungsansätze*, ed. Kerstin Dörhöfer (Freiburg, 1990).

true for children, who play an equally minor role in urban planning, and for people from other countries, who live in Germany but probably have very different needs in terms of public design due to their different cultural background.

In terms of these last two groups, our observations confirm this assumption: you can often see children playing football outside of dedicated play- or sports grounds using bicycle stands, lampposts, or benches as goals. The second observation regards city areas that are predominantly populated by people who spent part of their lives in Turkey. These older Turkish men (and women) seem to miss the usual benches in front of their houses and instead sit down on improvised seats, such as park barriers and low walls, in order to enjoy a neighbourly chat.

Let us return to the subject of gender-specific needs in public spaces. We want to demonstrate why public spaces could be interesting in terms of a gender-specific analysis. In our first proposition we have stated that public spaces are primarily designed by men without taking into account the needs of women, so that women have no other choice than to repurpose existing structures.

Our second proposition is based on the same idea of separation between male-dominated public sphere and female-dominated private sphere but leads to the opposite conclusion: The repurposing of existing structures is predominantly implemented by people who feel they are in their natural habitat, as it were, by people who feel "at home". So, if men feel more at home in public spaces thanks to centuries of male dominance in public life, is it fair to assume that men are responsible for the most changes of use? This assumption is confirmed by several studies, compiled by Maria Spitthöver, which show that the various areas in public spaces, such as streets, squares, parks, and sports grounds, are disproportionately more frequented by men than by women.[137]

This relates not just to use in terms of length of time, but also in terms of size of space occupied. On the basis of statistics regarding automobile use, Spitthöver demonstrates that roads are mainly used by men. This is because more men than women own a car, and the women who do own one usually drive smaller models.

An anecdote from the "Smart [car] Center" confirms that Spitthöver's 1990 study still carries some relevance today: A married couple, who had arrived in a Saab, were interested in the benefits of the small Smart car they were thinking of acquiring as a second vehicle. The husband reacted enthusiastically to the presentation by the saleswoman whereas the wife remained rather reserved. Eventually she remarked that it would be somewhat difficult to fit two children and the shopping in a two-seater car. The saleswoman replied that the idea behind the Smart was for her (the wife) to take the Saab when going shopping with the kids and for her husband to drive to work with the Smart. All of a sudden the husband seemed to have lost all of his earlier enthusiasm and the couple left rather quickly.

If men use public spaces more often, for longer periods of time, and more expansively, then we can assume that this will have a statistical effect on the number of instances of repurposing.

---

137   Cf. Maria Spitthöver, 'Frauen und Freiraum', in *Stadt-Land-Frau*, ed. Kerstin Dörhöfer (loc.cit.).

However, not only the quantity, but also the quality of use seems to indicate a prevailing male dominance in city traffic. During the summer, for instance, people tend to amble through shopping areas. Often, the following picture presents itself: pedestrians walk along the pavement in mainly gender-homogenous groups, and on the streets young men parade their cars by driving around in circles and listening to loud music in order to attract attention. This kind of behaviour, which implies a demonstrative use of the streets, can rarely be observed with women.

Another example is parking behaviour on multi-lane roads. Frequently people double park their cars, which can become a problem if someone whose car is parked closer to the pavement wants to leave but is blocked by another car that sits between theirs and the street. In many cases, the cars in the second row belong to shop owners who keep an eye on the situation from their shops, or can be alerted by sounding the horn. Sometimes, however, it happens that a car blocks another vehicle and its driver has gone shopping. The driver of the blocked car has no other option but to wait until the shopper returns. Very rarely this shopper turns out to be female.

It is harder to observe the people who implement changes of use than to observe the objects that are being repurposed. The reason for this is quite simple: the result of an instance of repurposing is visible for a longer period of time than the action of repurposing itself. A long-term empirical study would certainly be an important complement to the above-mentioned topics. On this occasion, we have to limit ourselves to assumptions and only a limited number of observations.

Out of the three activities of repurposing described in this chapter, that is sitting, providing information, and securing, not even the latter is easy to study with respect to gender-specific differences or similarities. Although it is easy enough to differentiate bicycles for men from the ones for women, we can no longer assume that they are used accordingly. Especially mountain bikes, of which there are a large number around, are often used by women. Our short-term observation, therefore, does not lead to particularly revealing results, since there is an approximately even distribution of bicycles for men and for women in public spaces. The same picture emerges when looking at bicycle stands and their alternative counterparts, such as barriers and street signs.

Sitting on objects that were not intended as seats, however, can be much more often observed with men than with women. This seems to confirm the proposition that men feel more at home in public and therefore stay there for longer periods of time and in more visible, demonstrative ways. Women, on the other hand, tend to use the streets in a transient way in order to get from one place to another. The sitting behaviour of groups, however, represents an exception: in these cases, we find far more women, and even more girls, who are sitting together while men usually sit on their own.

We assume that there are also gender differences when it comes to the application of notes, posters, and graffiti. More exact results, however, can only be obtained as a result of longer observation. Again, we believe that the confidence that men seem to possess in public spaces also results in a higher contribution to the "annotation" of a city.

We can summarise our observations regarding changes of use in connection with gender-specific aspects as follows:

- The separation between public spaces as a male domain and the private space as a female domain, which stems from the 19th century and still prevails today, suggests that the two sexes behave differently in public spaces and that they use the existing parameters in different ways.
- There are areas in public spaces which are used by everyone and there are those which are, or are considered to be, private property. Is it possible that instances of repurposing which take place in public spaces with somewhat private qualities are predominantly implemented by women since there is a stronger proximity (also in spatial terms) to the private sphere? An example in this context is the popular decoration of tree stumps with flowers, garden gnomes, and a certain type of note ("no dog toilet!").
- In public spaces, both public property (street furniture) and private property (items originating from the private sphere) are used. We assume that, in terms of gender, there is a difference in frequency and intensity when it comes to instances of repurposing for both object groups, because the first group belongs to the public sphere and therefore men are responsible for their existence and design, whereas the second group originates from the female-dominated private sphere.

Design between
Subject and Object

We have demonstrated that the relationship between the designed object and its use is a much closer one than many designers would tend to believe. It is in particular in those subconscious acts of repurposing that the intuitive connection between people and the objects that are surrounding them is expressed. This relationship can be disturbed through the intervention of design; it can, however, also be used as a basis for meaningful design. Let us return once again to the example of the chair: A chair whose backrest is designed in such a way that it is impossible to hang a jacket over it (for example Philippe Starck's coffeehouse chair "Costes") might be perceived as a nuisance.

We will now use a philosophical concept in order to demonstrate why design must not position itself as an obstacle between the user and the object and how, on the other hand, design can be applied to counteract this tendency. We will use Plato's concept of the world of ideas in order to demonstrate the nature of the relationship between design, object, and use. In this comparison Plato's philosophical intentions are of no significance whatsoever.

The Beautiful and the Good according to Plato

Plato's "ideas" represent the fundamental concept of his philosophy.[138] In the following, the term "idea" will be of central importance. However, since we will not employ the contemporary meaning of this term, but instead use it according to Plato's philosophy, let us first explain the difference: For Plato, ideas are the essence and the origin of things. Everything that exists is derived from ideas or archetypical images of which that thing is a part. Today, however, we use the term "idea" to signify individual possession. If someone has an idea it means that this person owns the idea. For professional designers, for instance, ideas are capital assets. If these ideas are meant to be sold, they have to be protected as soon as possible in order to avoid any potential theft. Once an idea is protected, nobody else is allowed to use it. Therefore, in contemporary language use, ideas are subjective.

For Plato, however, ideas are absolutely real and objective. They are not individual possessions but exist independently of humankind. They are eternal and constant. On the other hand, everything that exists in space and time, and can be experienced through the senses, is subject to change and transience.

Actual reality, therefore, is beyond space and time and can only be known through something other than sensual perception. According to Plato, the world of ideas is the world of true reality. Space and time, the so-called realm of representation, is not real in and of itself, but only in as far as it participates in the world of ideas.

The only connection that humans have with the world of ideas is the ability to create changing, transient representations thereof. So, for Plato, designers would be people whose profession is the creation of the best possible representations of universal

---

138 Cf. Rafael Ferber and Peter Sloterdijk, ed., *Platon* (Munich, 1998); ed. Anton Hügli and Poul Lübcke, *Philosophielexikon* (Reinbek bei Hamburg, 1991).

concepts. Designers do not have ideas, they have the ability to substantiate ideas and turn them into products.

In the context of NID-related issues, the platonic hierarchy of the Good and the Beautiful can serve as a model for defining objects according to their proximity to, or distance from, the concepts they are related to. Things that are considered beautiful, hence functional, are usually more transparent regarding the ideas that they represent.

When comparing objects which are used by many people in a non-intentional way with those which are rarely or never repurposed, a certain hierarchy can indeed be observed. Firstly, the things that are repurposed most often are those that display a low level of complexity such as boxes, glasses, chairs, or floors. At the bottom of the hierarchy, we find highly complex objects, such as electrical or electronic appliances.[139] Similar to Plato's model, we can use this hierarchy for the purpose of evaluation in the context of NID. Frequently referenced, low-complexity objects are closer to an archetypical image or idea than the rarely referenced, complex ones and are thus considered more beautiful, or better, from the perspective of NID.

From Idea to Object: Design

According to philosophical terminology, designers implement the idea of something that exists through a conscious, goal-oriented activity, thus creating phenomena which can be perceived through the senses. These phenomena are the designed objects.

This definition can be explained empirically using an example from our survey: the car mat that is used as a bathmat. During the design process, the concept of "something that lies between the feet and the floor" is turned into a phenomenon: a bathmat, a rug, or a car mat. Through an intentional, goal-oriented activity the concept is implemented in the form of an object. This comprises the aspects of essence and coincidence. The aspect of essence is represented through flatness, extension, and flexibility, altogether necessary characteristics of the object "mat". The different possible materials such as woven cloth for the bathmat, knotted wool for the rug, and rubber for the car mat are arbitrary attributes of the objects. In the case of the bathmat, and in addition to the different materials, size is another arbitrary attribute. Other objects would have different arbitrary attributes.

---

139   This is consistent with the results of our survey, in which none of those interviewed considered highly complex objects suitable items for NID. In this context, see also 'The Subjects: Objects of, and Reasons for, Repurposing'.

With no further modifications, car mats can take on the function of bath mats.

From Object to Idea: Non-Intentional Design

In product design, the designer selects specific arbitrary attributes in order to turn concepts into phenomena. Contrary to this, in creating NIDs people select different phenomena (objects) with specific arbitrary attributes because they recognise the idea behind the objects. They virtually see through the products.

Ignoring arbitrary attributes (such as material, size), they recognise the concept of "something that lies between the feet and the floor" in the bathmat, car mat, or rug. If they find themselves in the situation of needing something to lie between their feet and the floor, they can fall back on one of these three possible objects. If someone uses a car mat or a rug as a bathmat, then they have selected this item from a variety of existing objects (phenomena) with different arbitrary attributes because they have recognised the essence of a bathmat in the selected object.

Therefore, using a car mat as a bathmat represents a typical example of Non-Intentional Design. Although the activity itself is intentional and goal-oriented, it cannot be considered design when a car mat is used as a bathmat – this is NID. The precondition for an object to be considered a designed object is that it is derived from a concept that has been turned into a phenomenon; in other words, from a plethora of possible arbitrary attributes, a particular one was selected in order to combine it with the essence of a concept, and with the aim of creating an object.

We therefore have to differentiate between non-intentional activity and Non-Intentional Design. The activity by which NID is generated is indeed an intentional one, meaning it is carried out deliberately and in a goal-oriented manner. The result of the "transformation", however, is Non-Intentional Design because it is not concerned with the representation of a concept, therefore it is not design. Instead, an already existing design product is used because the idea behind it was recognised.

Design as Applied Philosophy

What's in a Name

In the discipline of design, a product is created from a concept. The less complex the product, the closer it is to the original concept or archetype. According to Plato, a chair would be a representation of the archetype "something to sit on". A chair, and a bench in a public space, for instance, are different representations of the same concept. There are, however, many more objects which, based on a (spontaneously arising) need to sit down, become representations of the concept "something to sit on": the edge of the bath, or that of a flower container, or the steps of a staircase. From a variety of available representations, people select the most suitable one in order to come closest to the concept of the archetype. The world of products offers a variety of options in this context.

For the products themselves, this means that naming them becomes crucial in relation to their use. Each object carries the name that it was given when it was created. People who buy a product also adopt its name even if they use the product for a different purpose. So someone who uses a chair predominantly as a clothes rack will still call the object a "chair" and not a "clothes rack". It seems fair to assume that people who refer to a chair used as a clothes rack as a chair when communicating with others have first completed a subconscious act of translation in order to enable communication about the object.

Even when these people are alone and are thinking about the object – for instance when they are tossing their clothes over it – they will, in all likelihood, still think of it as a chair and thus carry out an act of translation. Therefore, we can conclude that another precondition for generating NIDs is the ability to abstract terms from the objects they signify.

Certain objects are also renamed during use. These are predominantly objects that originate from a distant context and have very little relation to the actual situation. They might be very old, or might even be objects that are no longer being produced, or they might originate from another cultural context. There are things that "inherit" a redefinition of use over time. An example for this would be the use of milk churns as umbrella stands. We do not need milk churns any more since we buy our milk in cartons at the supermarket but numerous milk churns have been left from a time when they were needed. Using them as umbrella stands is quite common in rural areas. Interestingly enough the churns are called "umbrella stand" although they are clearly identifiable as milk churns. The change in use has, over time, created a change in nomenclature.

Consequently we can say that every object always has two meanings: the one that was given to it when it was designed, and the one it has received through use. The former always remains the same while the second might vary. A chair can be a chair-clothes-rack at one moment and a chair-ladder, or chair-chair, at the next.

Authority of Design – Autonomy in Use

Our attitude towards products is likely to change during use as well as during the design process. In order to create a better life with the products that surround us, it is important for both users and designers to question the authority of professional design and the naming of its products. For users, this is the basis for an independent use of existing products, and for designers it allows for a deeper understanding of possible uses and thus a deeper knowledge about what makes a product truly useful. NID as a specific form of use-related behaviour can provide the key to a useful design approach: Our survey and numerous individual discussions have shown that not only do people have the ability to use things differently, there is indeed a need for this kind of behaviour. The difficulties people had in terms of recognising that they had created instances of NID and, even more, of explaining their behaviour in terms of their actual motivations, has further shown that NID cannot be considered a deliberate act of design. For humans it is quite natural to use existing things around us, which today mainly means consumer products, in order to manage our lives. Consequently, NID is a potential that is inherent to all of us. Plato would say that all humans are able to recognise the concepts behind products, that is to see through the products themselves.

This last sentence is crucial to an open approach to design, an approach that allows the concept behind a designed product to shine through. This may sound trivial, it is, however, far from being common practice. Many things are designed in a way that obscures the archetypical concept from which they are derived. This is often due to the fact that the original concept is lost and replaced by another during the design process.

Non-Intentional Design as a Basis for an Open Design Approach

The significance of NID in the context of professional product design should not be underestimated: Following the analysis of behaviours of use in combination with Plato's philosophies on the world of ideas as a constructional tool, it has become clear that each object must be investigated from two opposing perspectives: from the perspective of design and from the perspective of use. In the design of products, designers follow a process that leads from the abstract to the concrete, hence from concept to product. When using products, users participate in the opposite dynamic: They are looking for a particular concept and on the way they will find products that best match this concept. If, during the design process, due consideration is paid to the fact that the reasoning behind future use will be diametrically opposed to that applied in the design process, then we can expect a qualitative and open design approach as a result. The way back from a concrete representation to the original concept must not be obscured, so that the autonomous use of products can be ensured.

Even if a product is so complex or so specialised that it is rendered unsuitable for ulterior uses, the product will still be more successful in terms of design appeal and sales if the concept behind it is obvious. In this context, the following rule applies: the more steps can be retraced from product to original concept, the more NID-suitable the product will be.

The opposite effect will be achieved with products that restrict autonomous use, and so tend to appear dictatorial, or seem to deny people's ability to recognise an underlying concept. Such products might be successful for short periods of time, but since they are usually subject to fashions they cannot be considered successful products in their own right. Among those badly designed products are those whose possible uses have been radically reduced through the application of explanatory decor. A mug which says "coffee" is very unlikely to make an appearance in the bathroom holding toothbrushes.

An authoritative design approach is particularly contraproductive in public spaces. These spaces are for everyone and therefore they should allow for individual interpretations of use, an aspect that should be embodied in the design of the objects placed in the public realm. A term that neatly captures the design quality needed in this context is fluidity. Fluid design provides a framework in which the object can communicate its meaning and usability. However, within this framework many interpretations are still possible. Objects that are designed on the basis of a fluid approach tend to suggest options of use instead of prescribing them. Both aspects are important, however. The most significant term in the context of public areas is "space": space for individual interpretations, space for thinking and movement, for encounters and communication.

The large variety of possible uses we have introduced for private and public spaces suggests that NIDs have had a longstanding history in the context of human problem-solving behaviour. At the same time, we are constantly developing new changes of use for new product groups. Conversely, NID ideas influence professional design approaches. This knowledge, however, seems to have got lost in contemporary product development. Intentional multi-functionality, semiotics, and increasingly bulkier manuals are proof that in professional design NID neither plays a significant role as a source of insight, meaning in a theoretical context, nor in the actual design of products itself, that is in a practical context. The logical conclusion is to transfer the knowledge of this innate human ability to professional design, in order to apply it, and put it to concrete use in the design of our future products.

In so doing, it is not our intention to create simple designs just because we are not able to think in complex ways, but because "complexity" is inherent in simplicity, and, most importantly, because a consideration of NID during the design process is bound to raise awareness for the empirical aspects of everyday life. This awareness will hopefully lead to a (self) reflection of some kind which is a precondition for the conceptualising and implementation of an open approach in design. NID as a method changes the perspective from which we view and evaluate the world of objects and thus represents an enrichment of our perception.

NID products are also interesting in terms of ecological considerations because they contribute to reducing an unnecessary overabundance of products. At the same time, multiple options of use tend to increase our appreciation of, and strengthen our relationship with, the respective products, which again results in an extension of their lifespan and saves resources. And last but not least, such products might save us a great deal of aggravation simply because we can use them in different ways. Who has not yet been annoyed by a chair that tends to roll away when we climb on it, or whose delicate wickerwork seat threatens to break while we are trying to change a light bulb? Including NID approaches in the development of products makes sense not just for economic but also for ecological, cultural and psychosocial reasons.

Bibliography

Agentur Bilwet: *Bewegungslehre. Botschaften aus einer autonomen Wirklichkeit*, Berlin 1991.

Albus, Volker; Borngräber, Christian: *Design-Bilanz*, Cologne 1992.

Albus, Volker; Winkler, Monika; Zeller, Ursula (Eds.): *Bewußt, einfach. Das Entstehen einer alternativen Produktkultur*, Bonn 1998.

Albus, Volker; Winkler, Monika; Zeller, Ursula (Eds.): *Anders als immer – Zeitgenössisches Design und die Macht des Gewohnten*, Stuttgart 2005.

Alexander, Christopher: *Notes on the Synthesis of Form*, Boston 1964.

Arendt, Hannah: *Vita activa oder vom tätigen Leben*, Munich 1967.

Assmann, Aleida: 'Die Sprache der Dinge. Der lange Blick und die wilde Semiose', in: Gumbrecht, Hans Ulrich; Pfeiffer, K. Ludwig (Eds.): *Materialität der Kommunikation*, Frankfurt (Main) 1988.

Attfield, Judy: *Wild Things. Material Culture of Everyday Things*, Oxford 2006.

autonome a.f.r.i.c.a. gruppe, Blisset, Luther; Brünzels, Sonja (Eds.): *Handbuch der Kommunikationsguerilla*, Berlin 1997.

Baacke, Rolf-Peter; Brandes, Uta; Erlhoff, Michael: *Design als Gegenstand. Der neue Glanz der Dinge,* Berlin 1984.

Ball, Ralph; Naylor, Maxine: *Form Follows Idea*, London 2005.

Baudrillard, Jean: *The System of Objects*, London and New York 1996 (1968).

Bausinger, Hermann: 'Die Botschaft der Dinge', in: Kallinich, Joachim; Bretthauer, Bastian (Eds.): *Botschaft der Dinge (= Catalogues of Museumsstiftung Post und Telekommunikation, 18)*, Heidelberg 2003.

Beck, Stefan: 'Die Bedeutung der Materialität der Alltagsdinge', in: Brednich, Rolf Wilhelm (Ed.): *Symbole: Zur Bedeutung der Zeichen in der Kultur,* Münster 1997.

Berger, Shoshana; Hawthorne, Grace: *Ready Made: How to Make (Almost) Everything*, London 2006.

Boehncke, Heiner; Bergmann, Klaus (Eds.): *Die Galerie der kleinen Dinge. Ein ABC mit 77 kurzen Kulturgeschichten alltäglicher Gegenstände vom Aschenbecher bis zum Zündholz*, Zurich 1987.

Bonsiepe, Gui: 'In der Phase des Prä-Design', in: *form 164*, 4/1998, p. 24/25.

van den Boom, Holger: *Betrifft: Design. Unterwegs zur Designwissenschaft in fünf Gedankengängen*, Braunschweig 1994.

Borngräber, Christian (Ed.): *Berliner Design-Handbuch*, Berlin 1987.

Bourdieu, Pierre: 'Die Ökonomie der symbolischen Güter', in: Bourdieu, P. (Ed.): *Praktische Vernunft. Zur Theorie des Handelns*, Frankfurt (Main) 1998.

Brandes, Uta: *Design ist keine Kunst. Kulturelle und technologische Implikationen der Formgebung*, Regensburg 1998.

Brandes, Uta; Erlhoff, Michael: *Non Intentional Design*, Cologne 2006.

Brandes, Uta; Steffen, Miriam; Stich, Sonja: 'Alltäglich und medial: NID – Nicht Intentionales Design. Die Dinge im Design', in: Ecker, Gisela; Scholz, Susanne (Eds.): *Umordnungen der Dinge*, Frankfurt (Main) 2000.

Brandolini, Andreas: *Kamingespräche. Designerinterviews und -monologe*, Kassel 1994.

Breidenbach, Joana; Zukrigl, Ina: *Tanz der Kulturen – Kulturelle Identität in einer globalisierten Welt*, Munich 1998.

Brock, Bazon: *Ästhetik als Vermittlung. Arbeitsbiographie eines Generalisten,* vol. III, Cologne 1977.

Brockhaus Enzyklopädie, Mannheim 1986.

Bulthaup, Gert: 'Die neue Küche: Lebensraum statt Arbeitszelle', in: *form 96/1981*, p. 11 ff.

Busch, Akiko: *The Uncommon Life of Common Objects. Essays on Design and Everyday*, New York 2005.

Burckhardt, Jacob: *Die Kunst der Betrachtung. Aufsätze und Vorträge*, Cologne 1997.

Bürdeck, Bernhard E.: *Design. Geschichte, Theorie und Praxis der Produktgestaltung*, Cologne 1991.

Chandrasekhar, Subrahmanyan: *Truth and Beauty*, Chicago 1987.

Chapman, Jonathan: *Emotional Durable Design. Objects, Experiences & Empathy,* London 2006.

Coleman, Roger (Ed.): *Design für die Zukunft. Wohnen und Leben ohne Barrieren*, Cologne 1997.

Cornfeld, Betty; Edwards, Owen: *Quintessenz. Die schönen Dinge des Lebens*, Munich 1987.

Cross, Nigel: *Designerly Ways of Knowing*, New York 2006.

Cultural Connections (Ed.): *Refuse. Making the most of what we have*, Toronto 1997.

Curtin, Deane W. (Ed.): *The Aesthetic Dimension of Science*, New York 1982.

Dery, Mark: 'Culture Jamming: Hacking, Slashing and Sniping in the Empire of Signs', in: *Open Magazin Pamphlet Series,* No. 25, 1993.

Designlabor (Ed.): *Öffnungszeiten. Papiere zur Designwissenschaft,* Issue 21/2007.

Dörhöfer, Kerstin (Ed.): *Stadt-Land-Frau, Soziologische Analysen, feministische Planungsansätze,* Freiburg 1990.

Doering, Hilde; Hirschauer, Stefan: 'Die Biographie der Dinge. Eine Ethnographie musealer Repräsentation', in: Hirschauer, Stefan (Ed.): *Die Befremdung der eigenen Kultur. Zur ethnographischen Herausforderung soziologischer Theorie,* Frankfurt (Main) 1997.

Dorschel, Andreas: Gestaltung. *Zur Ästhetik des Brauchbaren,* Heidelberg 2001.

Düllo, Thomas; Liebl, Franz: *Cultural Hacking. Kunst des strategischen Handelns,* Vienna 2005.

Elias, Norbert: *Über den Prozeß der Zivilisation,* Frankfurt (Main)1997.

Engelmann, Jan: *Die kleinen Unterschiede,* Frankfurt (Main)1999.

Erlhoff, Michael; Marshall, Tim (Eds.): *Design Dictionary,* Basel, Boston, Berlin 2008.

Ferber, Rafael; Sloterdijk, Peter (Eds.): *Platon,* Munich 1998.

Fischer, Ernst Peter: *Das Schöne und das Biest,* Munich 1997.

Flusser, Vilém: *Dinge und Undinge. Phänomenologische Skizzen,* Munich 1993.

Flusser, Vilém: *Vom Stand der Dinge,* Göttingen 1993.

formdiskurs. Zeitschrift für Design und Theorie, vol. 3, II/1997: 'Über Sprache, Gegenstände und Design'.

Friedl, Friedrich; Ohlhauser, Gerd (Eds.): *Das gewöhnliche Design. Dokumentation einer Ausstellung des Fachbereichs Gestaltung der Fachhochschule Darmstadt 1976,* Cologne 1979.

Fulton Suri, Jane & Ideo: *Thoughtless Acts. Observations on Intuitive Design,* San Francisco 2005.

Garner, Philip: *Schöner Leben (Catalogue),* Berlin 1983.

Gaver, William W.; Pennington, Sarah; Brendan, Walker: 'Cultural Probes and the value of uncertainty', in: *Interactions, XI. 5,* 2004, p. 53–56.

Gaver, William W.; Dunne, Anthony; Pacenti, Elena: 'Cultural Probes', in: ibid., VI. 1, p. 21–29, 199.

Giersch, Ulrich; Kubisch, Ulrich: *Gummi. Die elastische Faszination,* Berlin 1995.

Gomringer, Eugen; Spieker, Helmut: *Das Einfache,* published by Internationales Forum für Gestaltung Ulm, Gießen 1995.

Goodman, Douglas J.; Cohen, Mirelle: *Consumer Culture: A Reference Handbook,* Santa Barbara 2003.

Grass, Sibylle: *Zweckentfremdung. Äußerung des individuellen Konsums,* unpublished graduation thesis, Fachhochschule Nordwestschweiz, Hochschule für Gestaltung und Kunst 2005.

Grassi, Alfonso; Pansera, Anty: *Atlante del Design Italiano 1940–1980,* Milan 1980.

Gregotti, Vittorio: *Il disegno del prodotto industriale. Italia 1860–1980,* Milan 1982.

Groys, Boris: *Topologie der Kunst,* Munich 2003.

Guidot, Raymond: *Design,* Stuttgart 1994.

Hammer, Norbert; Kutschinski-Schuster, Birgit (Eds.): *Design und Identität,* Düsseldorf 1992.

Hartmann, Kiki; Nielsen, Dorte: *Inspired. How Creative People Think, Work and Find Inspiration,* Amsterdam 2005.

Hauffe, Thomas: *Fantasie und Härte. Das 'Neue deutsche Design' der achtziger Jahre,* Gießen 1994.

Hausen, Karin: 'Öffentlichkeit und Privatheit', in: *Journal für Geschichte,* vol. 1, 1989.

Hochschule der Künste Berlin (Ed.): *Objektalltag – Alltagsobjekte, Gestaltungsanalyse, Soziokultur, Geschichte,* Berlin 1988.

Hegemann, Michael: *Asthetik und Industrie-Design,* Munich 1992.

Helbrecht, Ilse: 'Der Wille zur 'totalen Gestaltung'. Zur Kulturgeographie der Dinge', in: Gebhardt, Hans; Reuber, Paul; Wolkersdorfer, Günter (Eds.): *Kulturgeographie. Aktuelle Ansätze und Entwicklungen,* Berlin 2003.

Heller, Martin; Windlin, Cornel: *Universal. Überall immer alles,* Zurich 1996.

Henne, Jurij; Neuman, Bastian; Schröder, Martin: *PC-Modding,* Bonn 2004.

Herles, Diethard: *Das Museum und die Dinge,* Frankfurt 1996.

Herterich, Frank: 'Urbanität und städtische Öffentlichkeit', in: Prigge, Walter (Ed.): *Die Materialität des Städtischen. Stadtentwicklung und Urbanität im gesellschaftlichen Umbruch,* Basel, Boston 1987.

Heubach, Friedrich Wolfram: *Das bedingte Leben. Entwurf zu einer Theorie der psycho-logischen Gegenständlichkeit der Dinge. Ein Beitrag zur Psychologie des Alltags,* Munich 1987.

Highmore, Ben: 'Das Alltägliche bewohnen. Zum Begriff des Alltagslebens bei Henri Lefebvre und Michel de Certeau', in: *Daidalos, 75,* 2000.

Hollein, Hans: *Design. MAN transFORMS. Konzepte einer Ausstellung,* Vienna 1989.

Hügli, Anton; Lübcke, Poul (Eds.): *Philosophielexikon*, Reinbek bei Hamburg 1991.

Hundsbichler, Helmut: 'Wörter und Sachen – Bilder und Sachen – Sachen und Menschen', in: Beitl, Klaus; Chiva, Isac (Eds.): *Wörter und Sachen. Österreichische und deutsche Beiträge zur Ethnographie und Dialektologie Frankreichs*, Vienna 1992.

Hutcheson, Francis: *An Inquiry Concerning Beauty, Order, Harmony, Design*, The Hague 1973.

IDZ Berlin (Ed.): *Design als Postulat am Beispiel Italiens*, Berlin 1973.

Jeggle, Utz: 'Vom Umgang mit Sachen', in: Köstlin, Konrad; Bausinger, Hermann (Eds.): *Umgang mit Sachen. Zur Kulturgeschichte des Dinggebrauchs (= 23. Deutscher Volkskunde-Kongreß)*, Regensburg 1983.

Jencks, Charles; Silver, Nathan: *Adhocism. The Case of Improvisation,* New York 1993.

Jonas, Wolfgang: *Design – System – Theorie*, Essen 1994.

Kähler, Gert (Ed.): *Geschichte des Wohnens. Band 4: 1918–1945 – Reform, Reaktion, Zerstörung*, Stuttgart 1996.

Kawakami, Kenji: Chindogu – *99 (un-)sinnige Erfindungen*, Cologne 1997.

Kepes, György (Ed.): *Der Mensch und seine Dinge*, Brussels 1972.

Klemke, Reiner E.: *Objektalltag – Alltagsobjekte. Bekleidung und Möbel der Familie K. Gestaltanalyse, Soziokultur*, Geschichte, Berlin no date.

Kluge, Andrea (Ed.): *Die Beliebigkeit der Dinge – anything goes*, Munich 1996.

Köhler, Gabriele: 'Städtische Öffentlichkeit und Stadtkultur', in: Dörhöfer, Kerstin (Ed.): *Stadt-Land-Frau, Soziologische Analysen, feministische Planungsansätze*, Freiburg 1990.

Koening, Giovanni Klaus: 'Tertium non datur, 1983', in: *Möbel aus Italien. Produktion Technik Modernität*, no place, no date.

Kremerskothen, Josef: 'Wegzeichen für eine Zeit, in der die Phantasie wieder eine Chance haben wird', in: *form* 96/1981, p. 8 ff.

Kron, Joan; Slesin, Suzanne: *High Tech – The Industrial Style and Source Book for the Home*, London 1980.

Krüger, Alfred: *Angriffe aus dem Netz (TELEPOLIS) – Die neue Szene des digitalen Verbrechens*, Munich 2006.

Kunsthalle Krems (Ed.): *Error-Design – Irrtum im Objekt*, Krems-Stein 1998.

Kunst- und Ausstellungshalle der Bundesrepublik Deutschland (Ed.): *Der Sinn der Sinne*, Bonn, Göttingen 1998.

Laurel, Brenda: *Design Research. Methods and Perspectives*, Boston 2003.

Lihotzky, Grete: 'Rationalisierung im Haushalt', in: *Das neue Frankfurt 5*, 1926/27.

Lüder, Dagmar (Ed.): *Das Schicksal der Dinge. Beiträge zur Designgeschichte*, Dresden 1989.

Mau, Bruce: *Life Style*, London 2005.

Mémo Larousse. *Encyclopédie générale, visuelle et thématique*, Paris 1990.

Meyers enzyklopädisches Lexikon, Mannheim 1971.

Molderings, Herbert: *Marcel Duchamp*, Frankfurt (Main) 1983.

Museum of Modern Art: *Italy – The New Domestic Landscape*, New York 1972.

Naylor, Trevor: *Living Normally,* London 2007.

Neue Gesellschaft für Bildende Kunst (Ed.): *Wunderwirtschaft – DDR-Konsumkultur in den sechziger Jahren*, Cologne, Weimar, Vienna 1996.

N.N.: 'An ihren Tüten sollt ihr sie erkennen', in: *form, Zeitschrift für Gestaltung*, 89/1980, p. 24 ff.

Norman, Donald A.: *Dinge des Alltags. Gutes Design und Psychologie für Gebrauchsgegenstände*, Frankfurt (Main) 1989.

Norman, Donald A.: *Emotional Design. Why We Love (or Hate) Everyday Things*, New York 2004.

Panati, Charles: *Universalgeschichte der ganz gewöhnlichen Dinge*, Frankfurt (Main) 1994.

Pettena, Gianni: *Superstudio. 1966–1982. Storie, figure, architettura*, Florence 1985.

Petroski, Henry: *The evolution of useful things. (How everyday artefacts – from fork and pins to paper clips and zippers – came to be as they are)*, London 1993.

Pontalis, Jean-Bertrand: *Objekte des Fetischismus,* Frankfurt (Main) 1972.

Porten, Dirk: NID – *Über die Entnormung der Dinge*, unpublished graduation thesis, Cologne International School of Design 2002.

Radice, Barbara: *Memphis Design. Gesicht und Geschichte eines neuen Stils*, Munich 1988.

Rentschler, Ingo; Herzberger, Barbara; Epstein, David (Eds.): *Beauty and the Brain*, Basel 1988.

Rudofsky, Bernard: *Architecture without Architects. A short introduction to non-pedigreed architecture*, New York 1964.

Ruppert, Wolfgang: *Fahrrad, Auto, Fernseh-schrank. Zur Kulturgeschichte der Alltagsdinge*, Frankfurt (Main) 1993.

Russo, Manfred: *Tupperware und Nadelstreif*, Vienna 2000.

Sack, Manfred: *Alltagssachen. Eine Sammlung von allerlei notwendigen Gebrauchsgegenständen*, Vienna 1992.

Sammlung Museum Boijmans van Beuningen, Rotterdam (Ed.): *Dinge*, Ostfildern 1998.

Sanderson, David W.: *Smileys*, Sebastopol 1997.

Saramago, José: *Der Stuhl und andere Dinge*, Reinbek bei Hamburg 1995.

Sato, Kazuko: *Alchimia*, Berlin 1988.

Schlögl, Markus: *Recycling von Elektro- und Elektronikschrott*, Würzburg 1995.

Schmidt-Bleek, Friedrich; Tischner, Ursula: *Produktentwicklung. Nutzen gestalten – Natur schonen*, Schriftenreihe des Wirtschaftsförderungsinstituts no. 270, Vienna 1995.

Scholz, Gudrun: *Die Macht der Gegenstände. Designtheorie. 3 Essays*, Berlin 1989.

Schönhammer, Rainer: 'Vom Umgang mit den Dingen', in: *Objekt und Prozeß*. 17. Designwissenschaftliches Kolloquium Burg Giebichenstein, Halle 1997.

Schönhammer, Rainer: Status, Luxus, Habitus. In: Hartmann, H.A. (Ed.): *Von Dingen und Menschen. Funktion und Bedeutung materieller Kultur*, Opladen 2000.

Schrage, Dieter: 'Das Objekt im Alltag', in: Drechsler, Wolfgang (Ed.): *Faszination des Objekts*, Vienna 1980.

Schwitters, Kurt: 'Merz', in: *Ararat* 19, December 1920.

Selle, Gert: *Geschichte des Design in Deutschland*, Frankfurt (Main), New York 1994.

Selle, Gert: *Siebensachen. Ein Buch über die Dinge*, Frankfurt (Main) 1997.

Selle, Gert; Boehe, Jutta: *Leben mit den schönen Dingen. Anpassung und Eigensinn im Alltag des Wohnens*, Hamburg 1986.

Siegel, David: *Web Site Design. Killer Web Sites*, Munich 1998.

Simmel, Georg: *Philosophische Kultur. Über das Abenteuer, die Geschlechter und die Krise der Moderne*, Berlin 1998.

Slater, Don: *Consumer Culture and Modernity*, Cambridge 1997.

Sommer, Carlo Michael: 'Der Lauf der Dinge. Aus der Sozialpsychologie der Alltagsobjekte', in: *Daidalos, 40*, 1991.

Spijker, Jakko van t': *Simply droog*, Amsterdam 2004.

Spitthöver, Maria: 'Frauen und Freiraum', in: Dörhöfer, Kerstin (Ed.): *Stadt-Land-Frau, Soziologische Analysen, feministische Planungsansätze*, Freiburg 1990.

Steffen, Dagmar: *Welche Dinge braucht der Mensch? Hintergründe, Folgen und Perspektiven der heutigen Alltagskultur*. Catalogue of the exhibition, Gießen 1995.

Steinbauer, Julia: *Nochmal besser. Aufwertung durch Umnutzung – Zweckentfremdung und Möbeldesign*, unpublished graduation thesis, Technische Universität Wien, Fak. für Architektur und Raumplanung 2006.

Tamás, Polgár: *Freax the Art Album*, Winnenden 2006.

Taut, Bruno: *Die neue Wohnung. Die Frau als Schöpferin*, Leipzig 1924.

The Encyclopedia Americana, Danbury 1985.

Thor, Alexander: *Das große Sicherheitsbuch – So schützen Sie Ihren Computer und Ihre Privatsphäre im Internet*, Berlin 2005.

Tsuzuki, Kyoichi: *Tokyo Style*, Kyoto 1993.

Turkle, Sherry: *Leben im Netz. Identität in Zeiten des Internet*, Reinbek bei Hamburg 1998.

Wagenfeld, Wilhelm: *Wesen und Gestalt der Dinge um uns*, Lilienthal 1990.

Werkbund-Archiv (Ed.): *Blasse Dinge, Werkbund und Waren 1945–1949*, Berlin 1989.

Wolf, Brigitte: *Design für den Alltag*, Munich 1983.

The Authors

Uta Brandes

Professor at the Cologne International School of Design (KISD) and free-lance (design) author. Studied English language and literature, sport, political sciences, sociology, and psychology. Professional appointments included: research assistant at the University of Hanover, deputy head of a research institute on gender issues in Hanover, deputy secretary of state in Wiesbaden, director of *Forum* at Bundeskunsthalle Bonn, director of Swiss Design Centre Langenthal, founding member and chairwoman of *Deutsche Gesellschaft für Designtheorie und -forschung* (German Association for Design Theory and Research), guest lecturer at design universities in Germany, Japan, Hong Kong, China, Australia, and the USA. Lives in Cologne.

Sonja Stich

Freelance designer in the areas of graphic design and exhibition design, works for clients from the cultural and publishing sectors. Carried out design-related research studies, worked for *frogdesign*, studied art history, Italian, and design in Münster and Cologne. Postgraduate studies in culture management. Lives and works in Bonn.

Miriam Wender

Designer and art director of the Milan-based new media agency *Infokiosk*. Formerly online editor of Italian design magazine *Domus*, founding member of Cologne-based new media agency *Apex-Netzwerk*, managing director of *Design Exchange GmbH* – the first European Internet-based design network. Lives and works in Milan.

Picture Credits

Chapter opening photos:

p. 6: Martì Guixé, 'Cau', Lighting with building-site lamp, Installation Fuori Salone 'Comfort & Light' for Danese, Milan, 2008

p. 18: Calamobio, Modernisation and revaluation of a fifty year-old commode through artistic design treatment of its surface, Alessandro Mendini, Zanotta, 1985/1988

p. 28: Andrea Brabetz, 'Dioniso's Ear', sculpture with newsprint, roccart '04 exhibition, Pietrasanta, 2004

p. 34: Matali Crasset, 'Bebox', jewellery box with brush bristles, DIM – Die imaginäre Manufaktur, 2000

p. 54: Pencil as letter opener

p. 104: Newspaper for stuffing into wet shoes

p. 122: Preserving jar as vase

p. 148: Barbara Caveng, 'Schirmherrschaft', umbrella made from plastic bags, 2008

p. 156: Cardboard box as lampshade

p. 176: Plastic bag as bib

p. 182: Shopping bag as wastebin

We would like to thank the following people and companies for kindly giving us permission to reproduce their images:

Albus, Volker, Frankfurt: p. 38 (6)
A.R.M. (All Recycled Material), Berlin (Photographer: Christian Reister): p. 47 (4–6), p. 148
Crasset, Matali, Paris, France: p. 34
Denzer, Maja, Barcelona: p. 127 (1)
Flos, Bovezzo, Italy: p. 37 (1)
Förster, Peggy, Cologne: p. 64 (2)
Foschi, Marcella, Cesena, Italy: p. 40 (8)
Freise, Andreas, Nordstemmen: p. 98 (1)
Frongia, Mattia, Florence, Italy: p. 40 (6)
Georgacopoulos, Alexis, Lausanne, Switzerland: p. 38 (5)
Hamm, Isabel, Cologne: p. 38 (4)
IFA CaseCon Championship, Berlin, http://ifa.dcmm.de: p. 93 (3–5)
Nochi, Cécile and Wyssem, Beirut, Lebanon: p. 38 (1–3)
Rafinesse & Tristesse, Berlin and Bern: p. 46 (1–3)
Szczepinski, Christoph, Kassel: p. 93 (1–2)
Zajonc + Partner GmbH, Breisach am Rhein: p. 95
Zander, Daniel, Cologne: p. 63 (6), 64 (1, 3), 65 (3–5), 68 (2), 69 (6), 70 (1, 3, 4), 71 (6), 72 (2, 4, 5), 73 (7), 76 (3, 5), 77 (11), 82 (5), 85 (2), 86 (1–2), 87 (1), 104, 114, 125 (1, 3), 127 (3–6), 165 (2, 3), 172 (3)
Zanotta SPA, Nova Milanese, Italy: p. 18, 21, 36, 37 (2, 3)
Zpstudio, Florence, Italy, http://www.zpstudio.it: p. 40 (7)

Images not expressly stated remain the copyright of the authors, Uta Brandes, Sonja Stich and Miriam Wender.

COPYRIGHTS

Design: Sonja Stich, Miriam Wender
Design Concept BIRD: Christian Riis Ruggaber, Formal
Typefaces: Akkurat, Arnhem
Translation from German into English: Susanne Dickel, Cologne
Project coordination: Karoline Mueller-Stahl, Leipzig

Library of Congress Control Number: 2008935484

Bibliographic information published by the Deutsche Nationalbibliothek
The Deutsche Nationalbibliothek lists this publication in the Deutsche Na-
tionalbibliografie; detailed bibliographic data are available on the Internet
at http://dnb.d-nb.de.

© 2009 Birkhäuser Verlag AG
Basel · Boston · Berlin
P.O. Box 133, CH-4010 Basel, Switzerland
Part of Springer Science+Business Media

Also available:
German edition (ISBN: 978-3-7643-8866-9)

Printed on acid-free paper produced from chlorine-free pulp. TCF ∞
Printed in Germany

ISBN: 978-3-7643-8867-6

9 8 7 6 5 4 3 2 1

www.birkhauser.ch